ELISE
CHRISTIE

RESILIENCE

ELISE
CHRISTIE
RESILIENCE

Reach Sport

For my grandmothers, Arlene Easson and Ann McCann, who continued to support me until their last breath.

Reach **Sport**

w w w . r e a c h s p o r t . c o m

Published in Great Britain and Ireland in 2021 by
Reach Sport, a Reach PLC business,
5 St Paul's Square, Liverpool, L3 9SJ.

www.reachsport.com
@Reach_Sport

Reach Sport is a part of Reach PLC.
One Canada Square, Canary Wharf, London, E15 5AP.

Hardback ISBN: 978-1-911613-63-3
eBook ISBN: 978-1-911613-64-0

Photographic acknowledgements:
Elise Christie personal collection, PA Images, Reach PLC.
Every effort has been made to trace the copyright.
Any oversight will be rectified in future editions.

Design and production by Reach Sport.
Written with Mark Eglinton.
Edited by Chris Brereton.
Design: Rick Cooke. Production: Michael McGuinness, Harri Aston

Printed and bound by CPI Group (UK) Ltd,
Croydon, CR0 4YY.

CONTENTS

ACKNOWLEDGEMENTS

WRITING A BOOK IS NOT SOMETHING I HAD ever really considered until I realised a few years ago that telling my story might help other people realise that not all battles are public.

As an elite athlete competing on the world stage, and having survived more than my fair share of sporting heartbreak, especially at the Olympic Games, some viewers think we are invincible, made of granite, emotionless machines who can switch off their thoughts and feelings as easy as flicking a switch.

It doesn't work like that.

As this book outlines, those in the public eye are no less human and no less immune to devastating life events – and subsequent mental health troubles – than anybody else.

I hope upon reading this book that you realise that the hardships some are going through can be completely unknown to the outside world, so kindness and understanding of others should be huge priorities for us all.

This book may not share all my battles but it does share an outline of my story.

Speaking of this book, I simply could not have done it without Mark Eglinton, whose patience, sympathetic ear and brilliant writing has helped bring my story to life. Thank you Mark.

Equally, publishers Reach Sport, especially Paul Dove and Chris Brereton, and my management team at Octagon have all worked extremely hard to ensure this book has come to fruition.

Nick Gooch is a man who looms large in the pages to follow and it was his guidance, his mentoring and his relentless drive for success that helped forge the athlete I am today. There are many other coaches who helped along the way, all of who deserve their own plaudits, and I thank you all for spotting something in me that was worth pursuing.

My family, especially my mum, also identified that if I was given the right guidance and encouragement then I had the opportunity to live a life, and participate in a sport, that would provide quite unbelievable highs and lows. I thank you too.

It has been quite a journey; a journey that is by no means over and a journey that continues to present its own challenges. I welcome them all. If life has taught me one thing – and it has taught me a lot, let me tell you! – it is that forgiveness is the key to success and that resilience, above all else, is a quality that can take you further than you ever dared dream.

Elise Christie, August 2021

PROLOGUE

I THOUGHT, *I'M DONE...*

And with that thought, the blade went in. As it did, I knew enough to understand that I was no longer myself, no longer Elise. I'd cut myself before of course, but that was different. The sting of pain from previous cutting escapades was temporary – intended simply to replace the emotional pain I was feeling at that moment with something more immediate. And it did that, for a while. A good cut could buy me a couple of hours of respite. Then the emotional pain returned, more hurtful than before and requiring a deeper cut to make it go away.

By December 2018 I'd reached a point in my life where I simply couldn't sweep everything under the carpet: the frustration because of injuries, the low self-worth, the constant financial pressures of being an athlete in a minority sport whose boyfriend had just dumped them by text message. Then there was losing Nick Gooch, my coach. It felt like there was nothing left in my life.

I'd just had enough, the inner pain was just too much and I was sufficiently desperate that I found myself upstairs at my house at midnight holding a razor blade against my left wrist.

I'd like to say that I know what my intention was that night, but I genuinely don't. There was no conscious thought whatsoever. Instead, it was as if I was watching myself in slow motion from above, powerless to alter the course of events playing out below.

I slid the blade deeper, much deeper than before, beyond the skin and blood and into something below that appeared to be white and... important. The blade cut through this white coloured object and I clearly saw the two halves fall away. Oddly, there was no pain.

What the fuck? Was that my vein? I thought, instantly returning to myself.

It is my vein... I'm going to fucking die.

One thing I knew right then was that I didn't want to die.

I shouted to my friend Brett for help. Thank god he was downstairs.

He loaded me into the front seat of his car and drove me to the hospital. On the way there I went through what I'd just done, over and over in my head. Why had I gone so much further this time? Was I trying to shock myself? Can I ever stop this?

This isn't normal, I thought.

ONE

SKELETON

THE THING IS, I DON'T THINK I HAVE EVER felt normal. Seriously, right from the start, my life has been quite weird.

Growing up in Livingston and going to school a few miles away in Edinburgh, by the time I'd reached primary three, by the time I was six or seven, I'd already experienced some physical bullying and had to move schools because of it.

On a daily basis at this first school, kids would come up to me and randomly shove me. Others would throw bits of plastic in my face for no reason.

Because I was so weak and timid, one time I fell, banged my head and split it open. I was so traumatised by it all that I couldn't go back. Every time my mum, Angela, tried to take me in I completely panicked. Eventually, she had no choice but to send me to another school.

I know now that I was bullied for the reasons that most people are: I was an easy target. At that age I was small and frail looking. Although in my own head I felt I was outgoing, the way others perceived me meant I didn't talk much and kept my head down. As a result, the air of weakness that surrounded me was probably like a magnet, pulling all the haters my way.

However, as much as I probably knew that being bullied wasn't normal, even at the age of seven, I'm not sure I gave it that much thought other than how to think of a way to stop it happening again the next day. I certainly had no idea how much impact it was going to have on me and I never considered the idea that it might inform every aspect of my life thereafter.

I also started exercising: running, dancing and figure skating initially, all at around the age of seven. Part of the reason for this early introduction was that my parents had split up when I was just six months old because my dad, David, was drinking too much. This left my mother to look after my elder brother Jamie and I on her own. I didn't have much of a close relationship with my dad at all when I was growing up.

As these familiar broken home situations often are, my mother's life with young kids was a day-to-day struggle. We lived in council houses. We never had much money and she had to work long hours to provide for us, which in turn meant that my brother and I quickly had to learn how to entertain ourselves when she wasn't around.

For years, Jamie and I looked after each other from a basic living perspective. He cooked for me and washed and dried my clothes whenever mum wasn't around; we were each other's only true friends for years. We're still very close nowadays because of it, albeit that we're very different and in no way understand each other's lives.

My mother had many admirable qualities and I would never for a moment question any of her parenting. But I do think, when I look back, that the reason she was so strict and controlling when she was around us was because she had this deep-seated fear that one day my brother and I might be tempted to drink like our father had in our later lives, or that we'd go down some other negative path.

Furthermore, I think there were two clear reasons why she was so pushy and why she forced me in particular into doing activities out of school at such a young age.

Firstly, again, she was so determined that I wouldn't get into trouble that her thinking became: if I were always occupied with something recreational, the chances of my stepping out of line would be that much reduced. It worked. Neither Jamie nor I ever did, we were too scared to! We were never allowed out after school and we weren't certainly allowed chocolate etc.

Secondly, I suspect she might have been living out some of her own lost ambitions through me. When she was younger, she'd been a talented athlete herself apparently. From all reports she was a really good long jumper. Unfortunately, at some point she ruptured her ACL and because knee treatments weren't as advanced as they are nowadays, the cartilage never fully recovered and she had to quit.

She has never herself said that her short athletic career was a motivator for pushing mine, but I've always had a suspicion that there's something in that theory. She wouldn't be exactly the first parent to live out their athletic ambitions through their kid.

With hindsight, my discipline as an athlete in later life was definitely borne partly out of this strict home life. No matter what I was told to do, I just did it. As much as we went without a lot of the time, my brother and I never missed what other kids had because we never had them in the first place. Jamie suffers from Asperger's Syndrome anyway. He finds it difficult to socialise and he just doesn't see life in the same way as others do. Consequently, when he was a kid he was always more withdrawn and solitary in social situations than when he was with me at home. And even when he was at home, he was into activities that required quiet thought, like chess and computers – and of course preparing for his classes at school.

I was the complete opposite. Apart from dancing (which I'm still absolutely shocking at nowadays, by the way) I was a natural, albeit a reluctant one, at whatever physical endeavour I was pushed towards. I did fine in the classroom and worked hard enough to get by.

But I did even better outside of it.

I can clearly remember the first time I ever stepped onto

ice – it was at Murrayfield Ice Rink in Edinburgh and I was seven years old. It was one of those occasions where a friend had gone skating once or twice and their mum asked mine if I'd like to go too. I certainly don't remember there being any strong wish on my behalf to go skating. I wasn't active by choice. I just thought, *why not?*

Normally, when anyone, far less a young kid, first sets foot on an ice rink, they stumble around, arms flailing at their sides, trying to stay upright. We've all seen it; most of us have done it. It's kind of an ice-walk, and often involves clinging onto the side barrier for dear life at some stage.

I never did any of that. I just walked onto the ice, totally fearless, pushed off and skated away. I never gave it a second thought. It was as if I already knew how to skate. From there I just got better and better. Before long I started figure skating properly and my mum was pushing me to keep going, I began wanting to be better than anyone else at it.

The skating club at Murrayfield at that time was run by Diane Dewar, who herself was a highly experienced ISU figure skating coach who'd been at several World Championships. She had a proven track record of identifying young talent, nurturing it and then developing it to elite level.

Initially, it was another lady in the club, Fiona Richardson, who coached me for the first couple of sessions. As much as I could stay upright, I was an absolute beginner. But I was making progress and becoming more comfortable each time I ventured onto the ice.

Then, one day, Diane herself saw what I was doing and I

guess you could say she kind of tried to poach me – which I remember feeling, even at that age, was a bit of an awkward position to be put in for a kid.

"What do you want to do?" my mum said.

"I'll just go with Diane," I said, not really knowing what the right answer was.

In the end, and with no disrespect meant to Fiona who is also an excellent Level 2 coach in her own right, it was the right decision for me. Within a short period of time Diane brought her great experience to bear. Along the way she taught me an awful lot about the concepts of commitment to a sport and training hard, all at an age where I was highly receptive to her guidance and passion.

It was also her that enlightened me about the foundations of skating in the most holistic of ways. Not only was I getting a solid grounding in the mechanics of the sport, but I was also being exposed to a degree of understanding of the more nuanced aspects like how the body *feels* in certain circumstances when you're trying to control it and move in a certain way, and why.

Although I didn't understand it at the time, both of these types of knowledge are vital to being a great skater. The very best can do and feel, and I carried this understanding she instilled in me forward without ever really thinking about it again. Simply, I became a natural. In every sense Diane was such an inspiring woman, without whom I wouldn't be where I am today.

And let's face it, I needed all the inspiration I could get

because, when I went to high school, the bullying I'd been enduring not only continued but was now of a different kind.

Instead of pushing and hitting me, it was more of an emotional and psychological type of abuse. While I didn't have my head split open again, I might as well have. The torment was no easier to deal with. While it left no visible scars, the new type of abuse tore me up inside.

Looks were still the issue. At that age, as young teenagers, the girls around me were starting to wear makeup, do their hair and be fashion aware. As you can imagine, the school hallway became this hormone-fuelled bitchy world where everyone was analysed, judged and, ultimately, picked upon relentlessly until they either conformed or broke. Believe me, people think teenage boys are competitive; girls are every bit as bad.

The problem was, I wasn't motivated by any of my immediate peer groups' interests. Because I was engaged in sport every day, I had no fashion sense other than tracksuits and training shoes. Because I was always training and inevitably in and out of showers afterwards, I didn't wear any makeup, I had no time to dry or style my hair and I was just crudely scraping my hair back or hiding it in my clothes. I was just a total tomboy, as hard as my mum tried to convince me to change.

As if being the odd one out from a fashion sense didn't make me a big enough target, my body shape didn't help much either. As much as I was exercising, I was still thin and not very muscular at all. As fit and healthy as I might have been, these physical traits only made me stand out more from the other girls, many of whom I could see were transitioning into semi-adult, female versions of themselves with growing breasts, feminine curves, and all the unpredictable hormonal fluctuations that go along with that confusing period in any girl's life.

In summary, everyone said I wasn't 'girlie' enough. And in the absence of anything else to call me, they all just kept calling me 'skeleton'. It became a relentless cycle of daily name-calling torment. Whatever I did and wherever I went, skeleton followed me for the duration of every school day and because I was training in the evenings after school – and everyone knew that – they just picked on me even more.

Only occasionally did I even try to stand up for myself. But it was, ultimately, futile. Whenever I tried to justify my appearance on the fact that I was an athlete, they accused me of lying about being an athlete in the first place. I couldn't win. I was just miserable.

There were too many girls ganging up on me at once. As small a minority as it probably was in real terms, in my head it felt as if the weight of public opinion in the school was already against me and was sizeable, which, on reflection, could have been seen as the shape of things to come.

Given how young I was, I had no idea how to understand how I was feeling at this time. I kept out of the way of people and situations at school, other than sticking with the only two friends that I'd known since primary school.

At home, because my mum had to work so much, I had nobody to talk to about anything, if I'd even wanted to. I'd lock myself away in my room when I wasn't skating – not that my brother and I were allowed to leave the house anyway. The idea of a boyfriend never even entered my head.

For the first time, as I isolated, I started becoming very critical of myself and I've never really stopped since. In some senses this depth of self-analysis has helped me in my skating career, in others it has made life hell.

But back then when I was sitting in my room at night stewing, there were just no positives that I could see. Each night, I would go through the same pointless cycle of analysing what people had said about me at school that day in detail, and then I'd go over it again and again in my mind.

Before long, I'd convinced myself that these girls were all right about their criticisms of me. In turn, I started judging and denouncing every single aspect of myself too: my abilities, my voice, my body, my hair, my face, my teeth – everything. I started seeing only imperfections. The more I saw, the harder on myself I became.

Anxiety absolutely took over to the point that I couldn't be around people. *I'm not good enough*, I kept telling myself.

I badly needed a lifeline, and soon I found one.

Skating became everything, and thank god that it did.

With athletic pursuits generally, at first I had just been doing as I was told by mum, and then letting whatever small amount of desire I had to be better at each push me along.

However, things were changing. This time it was personal. With all the background torment in my school life sucking me into a miserable vortex, I started feeling some momentum of my own to use skating to pull me out of it.

Up until the age of around 13, the sole focus had only been on figure skating and it wasn't long before I was good at most aspects of it on the back of my disciplined attitude to training – most of which took place at an ice rink in East Kilbride under Diane Dewar's care.

I liked some aspects of figure skating and disliked others. I seemed to have some sense of critical instinct, even at such a young age. Because of Diane's teaching, I was always a good technical skater on the ice, and before long I was also skilled at using edges and carving with the blades. Also, because I was athletic, I found that I could jump well and could land all the complicated triple jumps that were required to excel at the discipline. Those aspects were the likes.

But there's much more to figure skating than jumps, and I just wasn't cut out for the more theatrical, dance-orientated performance fluff that had to happen in between these occasional extravagant leaps. I was useless at that part. I was always so floppy-handed and inelegant. So, I'd jump, skate around a bit for a while – then I'd just do another jump. Let's just say I didn't score very good points for artistic impression.

Because I was still so timid and self-conscious, it got

to the point where I really hated performing in front of an audience. I wasn't enjoying the competition of figure skating either and I just didn't suit the scene. I felt like a clown, and not a very good one.

And then the big break came that would ultimately transform my life.

At the age of 13, I was able to get on the ice to try speed skating for a change because a new facility had recently opened in Prestwick called the Centrum Arena.

The plan there was for it to become a national, centralised skating venue and ice hockey rink for the Ayr Scottish Eagles in the winter months, similar to the National Centre in Nottingham. In the summer, the same space was to be used for other recreational events like the Chinese State Circus and concerts. However, the best thing about Centrum was that it could accommodate a full size short track rink.

I can't tell you how significant the timing of this was, especially when I also tell you that one of the biggest problems in British speed skating has always been the lack of facilities at which to skate, far less race.

Back in 2004/2005, until Centrum opened, there was quite literally nowhere to speed skate. As much as we could skate recreationally doing figure at Murrayfield, Stirling and East Kilbride from time to time, none of those venues had the capability to house a full size short track rink. However, Centrum opening was the stroke of luck I needed at the right time.

Now that I had joined a club, the next issue was the

other one that pretty much plagues speed skating in the UK even to this day: where to race.

As much as anyone can learn basic techniques and therefore become a proficient technical skater, the only way you learn to race in a sport that is absolutely defined by the act of racing, is quite simply to race as often as possible.

You can theorise about it all you want and watch as many videos of other people racing as you can lay your hands on. You'll learn something that way for sure – but until you actually get on the ice and feel what it is to be in a race with other people thinking like you, you're just not going to improve.

What was especially frustrating was that other countries seemed to be managing it just fine. In Canada, kids are introduced to the ins and outs of racing almost as soon as they can stand on blades. In China and South Korea it's similar. Even in some European countries like the Netherlands and Italy, they start them very early.

However, even today, in 2021, short track is still a minority sport in the UK that has insufficient opportunities to race. Even today, in 2021, I, a multiple medal winner and former world champion and part of a national organisation like Team GB, still struggle at times with that perennial issue of getting access to ice. It's crazy, but that's how it has always been with speed skating in Britain.

I should probably explain, for anyone that doesn't know: short track speed skating takes place on an oval track. The standard distances for competition are 500m, which is 4.5

laps, 1000m, which is 9 laps and 1500m, which is 13.5 laps. Additionally there are relay distances that are comprised of 3000m races for women and 5000m for men.

While all tracks are the same regulation size, because of variations in the condition of the ice, not all tracks behave exactly the same way. Regardless of ice condition, the lane you're in makes a lot of difference. In a 500m race it's normal to have four skaters in a race, each of them in a lane that's numbered 1-4, with 1 being the inside and 4 on the outside.

Obviously, given that the track is an oval, the inside of the track is the shortest way round it and the outside is the longest (the difference is approximately 30m per circuit, which is a massive amount).

To that end, with energy at an absolute premium, it's important to make sure that you're not expending more than others in the race by having to go wider unnecessarily.

Sometimes passing on the outside is unavoidable however, and is the only way to win a race. If you're stronger than everyone else in a race, you're better placed to be able to pass.

But generally, you'll mostly see someone getting off the start in front, and the others sitting in behind in the slipstream, albeit each will take what's called a different 'line' into each bend – a line being the angle taken into and out of a curve to maximise speed and efficiency.

From an equipment perspective, it's all highly technical and no less scientific. I suppose you could say that the skates themselves are less critical than the blades mounted on the bottom of them. These blades are vital in terms of allowing a skater to both carve into corners at high speed, but also to generate high speed on the straight sections of the track.

Different blade compositions and different blade set-ups can be tailored to suit every nuance of a skater's technique and style. And everyone is slightly different, albeit that the fundamental technique required to move efficiently in short track is fairly standard.

Before long, I was doing speed skating training on the ice at least twice a month and getting steadily better at it under the guidance of a new group coach called Archie Marshall. Within a matter of weeks I'd forgotten all about figure skating.

There were, however, a few basics to address at the start. The main problem people have when switching from figure skating to speed is that normally they bounce as they move. Indeed, in figure skating, you're actually taught to push through your toes and to bounce up and down as you move. This bouncing action is necessary to create the required speed on the ice.

In speed skating the approach to forward movement is completely different. Instead of bouncing, you've got to stay down and in a compact position with your weight forward. From here you only push through your heels and in turn the quads and glutes become vital components for doing all the work. This combination of posture and muscle groups is where your speed and power comes from in speed skating.

Once you've mastered the basic motion, you're only

halfway there. You've got to be able to learn the subtleties of edge-work, which is vital both for gaining speed on the straights and for turning corners on the rink at high speed.

Obviously, in a short track rink that's only 110 metres around, these straight parts are what you'd call very long. In fact, when you're on a track, it always feels like you're turning.

However, these straights are important because it's here that you've got to generate the speed and the position that will allow you to take the appropriate line into a corner. And to do this you must roll from the inside edge to the outside edge of your skates as you move. The better you are at controlling this through your ankle, the faster you'll go.

Luckily for me, given my experience with figure skating, I wasn't a total beginner in the sense that I could already use both edges – inside and outside – to move. Very quickly, at these Centrum sessions under Archie's guidance, I was learning all of these subtleties and more.

Without really analysing it too much, I was transitioning fully into becoming a speed skater. Better still, I liked it, I was good at it, and I could tell that it played to my physical and mental strengths much more than the more theatrical based aspects of figure skating.

With hindsight, the honest truth is that figure skating had been just too subjective for my liking. There was way too much emphasis on vague concepts like impression and art to appeal to a facts-driven tomboy like I was.

Conversely, with its winner-takes-all, roller-derby

sensibilities, speed skating simplified everything for me as a shy teenager. Instead of being out there on the ice alone, with an audience of mothers and teenage girls watching my every move and my every awkward ballet pose, all I had to do was line up elbow to elbow, head to head with four or eight others at the start, wait for the go instruction and then push off hard.

In addition to speed, which I always liked, there were also race tactics and an ever-present potential for falls and collisions. For someone who'd had a tough time standing up for herself to that point, I won't deny that the more combative aspects of speed skating very much appealed to my teenage self.

The best part of speed skating was that it was fact based in the sense that the only measurement of success was totally objective: whether I crossed the winning line first or not. And the first time I did, at one of the very infrequent races in those very early days, I won a selection box of chocolates. As it was handed to me, I remember thinking, *I could get used to this!*

Let me tell you, for someone who was never allowed any sweets, that prize was all the incentive needed to keep going!

When Centrum closed (and it's now a Sainsbury's) I started being looked after on a more personal athlete-to-coach level by a speed skating coach called Brian Reid from the Forth Valley Speed Club based in Stirling. Brian was slightly built, quietly spoken yet – given he'd been a competitive international skater himself – with a steely determination in his eyes

I'd met Brian at some of the infrequent race weekends I'd been to, and he clearly recognised my talent to the extent that he soon became a much more personal, one-on-one coach. Like Diane and Archie, Brian was another vitally important figure in my young skating life without whose enthusiasm I certainly wouldn't have had the career I have had.

Brian was the kind of person that you'll find at sports clubs throughout the country, and he's the type of unsung hero that every amateur sports club desperately needs. Even I could tell that the club didn't have much by way of resources, but he more than made up for that by being willing to give up so much of his own time to turn up at all hours to suit me, to train me off the ice.

In his capacity as the coach of my first proper speed skating team, Brian was not only prepared to race me up flights of stairs to get me aerobically fit, but he was also the one who taught me the absolute basics of how to be competitive from a speed skating standpoint. Brian did everything he possibly could for me with what little means he had and I'll forever be in debt to him for that investment he made. It's so sad to see that he's suffering from MND nowadays and is no longer able to coach or skate.

Meanwhile, even though I'd shown a winner's edge, my mother continued to be quite hard and critical towards me.

Whenever I fell on the ice, she'd tell me off, "Elise! What

are you doing?" To which I'd say, "But I didn't mean to fall!" "Get up, go again!" she'd shout. Equally, it's fair to say that whenever I did do well, she did at least give me some praise.

What I understood even then was that, while she was definitely much tougher on me than other mums were on their kids, she was only like that because she felt that she'd given me this opportunity, could see that I had talent, and therefore she only wanted me to see it through as far as I possibly could because she herself had missed out.

There inevitably came a time where it became less about my mother and more about me. As I became better at this new discipline of speed skating, it gradually dawned on me that while it had been my mother pushing me previously and I'd been happy to just go along with it, I was now propelling myself, and for different reasons,

For the first time in my young life, I'd found something that not only was I good at but that also allowed me to escape myself for the time I was on the ice. While I was out there moving at speed with the air rushing past my helmet feeling pure, unadulterated bliss, I also had total freedom from the negative commentary that was running in a tedious loop in my own head: the questions, the doubts, the self-criticisms, the, *Elise… you're no goods.*

On the ice I *was* good, that much I knew. And from that moment on, with something tangible to separate the two distinct and conflicted parts of me, I was ecstatic. For the first time I was in charge, and I did it all with a confidence and willingness to take calculated risks in speed skating races that I just didn't have off the ice.

The bizarre thing about all of this is that even then, as much as I was training like an athlete in terms of my discipline and my mindset in my teens, I still wouldn't say that I personally had any thoughts of *being* an actual athlete at all – certainly not for a career.

The truth is, I was already one of the best in Scotland and I'd got there not by thinking about where that might take me, but by simply beating whoever was put in front of me at any given moment. It wasn't in any way scientific or calculated; I certainly didn't have any aspirations to be the best in the world or even an Olympic athlete at all.

If anything, at the age of 15 I suppose I still just wanted a traditional life. My disciplined attitude to skating went hand in hand with a diligent approach to the classroom. I'd passed all my exams and I suppose I still saw university as my route forward, possibly to become an aircraft technician, which for some reason was my idea of a dream job at that time.

Beyond that I think I also wanted to get married and have kids. More than anything though, and as much as I didn't always feel it, I just wanted to be normal.

TWO

ODD SHOES

AS ABSOLUTELY GUTTED AS MY MUM WAS when I got the chance to move to Nottingham at the age of 15 to become part of the national team performance programme, it's important to know it was her that made the decision for me to go in the first place! In a way it made her even more attached to me because I wasn't there.

At this point, I was adamant that I didn't even want to do it. As much as I was training hard, skating at weekends and was clearly good at it, when I came second in the 2005 short track British Championships in Sheffield because of a penalty in one of the race disciplines, I was discouraged to put it mildly.

As was already my way, I was pretty brazen on the ice that day. By that time, I was dropping (short track terminology for leaving an opponent far behind in your wake) everyone left and right in races. Nobody was ever near me.

Anyhow, in the final I went round the outside of this girl with three laps to go and when I did so she just kind of fell over. I didn't actually touch her, but they gave me a penalty anyway. I remember there being this big uproar about it at the time.

I was furious. I should have won, but I didn't. Even back then, as a scrawny teenager, I just didn't *do* second place. Beyond the frustrating issue of the highly suspect disqualification itself, I saw zero point in doing something if I wasn't the absolute best at. In the days immediately after those British Championships, in my head I was basically done with skating.

Instead, having passed my exams and having already started looking into the idea of going to university, I began planning a life outside of skating and, in fact, outside of any sport.

Then the phone rang. I was sitting in my bedroom and I heard my mother shout up from downstairs.

"They want you to join the national team!" my mum said.

Apparently skating wasn't done with me. Although I'd lost at the British Championships, my potential hadn't gone unnoticed.

"I'm not doing it," I said, without even looking up.

"But you'd be in the *national team*!" she repeated.

"I don't want to go. I hate sport and I'm going to university," I said.

With hindsight, I'd learned enough during my weekend exposure to short track events to get a real sense and idea of where the sport sat in the country's list of priorities.

In those days, pre the 2012 London Olympics, it felt to me as if Great Britain didn't take sport very seriously and therefore didn't win anything. There just didn't seem to be a culture in place that raised winners and won medals. I just thought, *why would I want to join the national team if there's no chance of ever winning a medal?*

These were, of course, the misguided, inaccurate assessments of a 15-year-old who, because she'd lived a very protected life to that point, was probably equipped with the mental age of no more than that of a 12-year-old. The truth of the matter was that I really didn't know what I was talking about, but I was adamant I wasn't going all the same. In the end, my mother made the decision for me.

"You're going. You'll regret it later in life if you don't," she told me.

Again, I think she thought she was acting in my best interests. On one hand, I'm absolutely certain that it was a huge wrench for her to pack her innocent little waif-like daughter off into the big, bad world at such a young age.

However, given her own experiences with her own athletic career, I just think she was wary of me turning around a decade later when I was more mature and worldly and throwing it all back in her face in a, "Why didn't you make me go?" kind of way.

Instead, she just made me go – literally gave me no choice whatsoever. She packed all my belongings in a suitcase, loaded them in the car and drove me to Nottingham. I hardly had any time to complain about it. I was becoming a career athlete whether I liked it or not. I just went along with it.

In retrospect, the decision to move away from home at such a young age was one of the best things that ever happened to me. Few 15-year-old girls were more clueless about the realities of the world than I was in August 2006. I badly needed to grow up, and being unceremoniously dumped in the middle of Nottingham with a suitcase was definitely the best way of forcing me to do it.

In the initial days and weeks, I was inevitably wandering around a new city like an absolute airhead thinking, *so what are we actually doing here?*

But gradually, in a different place among different people far away from my mother, I started finding my feet.

I was accommodated with what was called a host family. That description perhaps suggests something quite comfortable and homely but, in truth, it was just someone who was willing to take responsibility for me on a basic level.

My host was a figure skating coach, and the house was in a residential area, don't ask me its name, within a long walk's distance of the Nottingham National Ice Centre. With a roof over my head for when I wasn't skating, it was very much, "There's the kitchen, that's the bathroom. Get on with it."

Suddenly, literally a day after leaving Scotland, there I was in a strange house with people I didn't know, in a different country. As someone who'd been used to being at home with my mum and Jamie, I won't deny that it was all a bit awkward to begin with. As friendly as the host was, I never felt especially comfortable with the idea of roaming around in some stranger's home.

I think, from what she's said since, that my mum was promised things that didn't happen: that I'd get proper cooking lessons etc. But I can promise you that those didn't ever transpire. I got a little basic help from my host in terms of how to be an adult, but I still had no choice but to learn how to swim in that first year or else the alternative would have been to sink.

By that point I had literally never cooked anything in my life. Whenever we'd needed to eat anything at home when my mother wasn't around, my brother Jamie would just put in a supermarket pasta box or such like. Overnight, I had to figure out how to buy food, how to cook it and whatever else an independent person has to know how to do.

In a wider sense, it was all such a massive lifestyle change to go from a small town in Scotland, where I wasn't allowed to do anything at all, to a medium sized city in England where I could literally do whatever I wanted. For any teenager this all would have been a culture shock. But for me, the most smothered of all 15-year-olds; it was like I'd landed from another planet.

I clearly remember walking back to the house from the centre during the first month or two. On one hand I felt liberated to be able to do it at all – to be walking along a street at my own pace with nobody checking where I was and when I'd be home. On the other I had the first realisation that there was a dangerous world out there I'd had no knowledge of previously.

These places were unfamiliar. Equally, the faces and voices were so alien too. I had no idea what any of the areas in Nottingham even were. I'm not even sure I knew what area I was living in but I knew enough to recognise that it was a little rough.

That night in question – as I was walking home alone in the dark – this car pulled up alongside me and this threatening-looking man got out of it and started talking to me. As I understood it, he wanted me to get in the back of his car. I had no idea what to do. I was a kid, miles from home. I had no experience of situations of that kind. I stood there frozen to the spot.

Feeling my phone weighing in my pocket, I acted instinctively as he moved towards me and pulled it out and started talking as loudly as I could. The man backed off, got in his car again and drove off. I have no idea what his intentions were, but I'm pretty certain that they weren't good. It was all such a wake-up call.

As much freedom as there was on the outside in Nottingham, life in the national team training programme was anything but free.

Under the tutelage of national head coach Nick Gooch, who'd be my coach for many years thereafter, I was one of about 25 athletes ranging in age from me, the baby of the group at not quite 16, to the oldest athletes who were probably in their early thirties at the time.

Every day we were told what to do, when to do it and what to bring. No amount of deviation from that was acceptable. Everything about our daily lives was organised and disciplined. And fortunately, given the way my mother had forced my brother and I to live, being a disciplined athlete came very easily to me.

However, at the outset, I felt like I was right back at school. I definitely felt like I was the outsider in a group all over again.

Although I naturally gravitated towards two other girls in the group, Charlotte Gilmartin (Upcott is now her married name) and Sarah Lindsay, even then I always felt so much younger than they were, which in Sarah's case was true given that she's 10 years older than me and was the experienced girl in the group, having been to the 2002 Winter Olympics in Salt Lake City and the 2006 Games in Turin.

It wasn't even a matter of maturity in numerical terms that set us apart really (Charlotte and I were both born in 1990), but more of that lack of worldliness on my part that I described.

The fact of the matter was that most of the others in the group had either lived in a city or had at the very least been exposed to one and were a little streetwise because of it. They knew how to get places, how to use public transport and the general dos and don'ts of urban living. I, on the other hand, was from Livingston, and was the absolute opposite of streetwise. I immediately felt as if I was at a disadvantage in the group because of that.

Consequently, Charlotte and Sarah helped me a lot through that first season and my god did I need it. Sarah taught me how to cook; Charlotte taught me how to get around. Between them, they dragged me up to closer to their level of street smarts pretty quickly and I'm so grateful to them for that help. For a while there I was truly disorganised – to the extent that on more than one occasion I showed up at training in the morning with odd shoes on.

"You've got one Umbro and one Adidas, Elise!" Sarah told me, as I walked into the changing room half asleep one morning.

"What? Oh really. I didn't notice," I said.

It took a couple of months at least for me to find my place in the group, even though a shared experience that could be judged in inarguable factual terms – how good a speed skater you were – helped make the national programme a much easier place to get acceptance for me than school ever had been.

Ever since I started speed skating, which relies much more on physicality than figure skating, I'd always had good technique in the sense that I inherently knew how and with how much force my skate blades should interact with the ice.

Not only that, I could also look at someone else skating

and know exactly what they were doing right and, perhaps more importantly, what they were doing wrong. I have no idea how I knew any of this right from the start. Nobody taught me it; it can't be taught anyway. It must have been all instinct.

However, as good as I was technically, when I compared myself to the others the most glaring revelation for me was how far behind everyone I was when it came to fitness.

This conditioning gap really set us apart in these early weeks and months.

Aerobic fitness in speed skating is everything. No matter how good your technique is, if you're not fit, your technique will fall apart, which mine certainly did in those early weeks.

The reason for this was, again, related to simple geography. Because all of the rest of the group were from England, almost all of them had come from club situations whereby they'd probably been training two or three times per week on the ice, never mind what else they'd been doing off it.

Meanwhile, there I was, down from Scotland, where I was lucky if I had a proper formal speed skating training session more than twice a month after Centrum closed.

Initially, this differential was so glaring that, for all that my solid technique could carry me so far, because I was so relatively unfit most people in the group were half lapping me over 500 metres. It was embarrassing.

Fortunately, while not everyone can acquire good technique or have an eye for the nuances of a skate on ice, fitness is something anyone can develop if they're willing to work hard enough, and I definitely was in those first few months in Nottingham

I pushed myself above and beyond to get fit. No way was I prepared to let myself be shown up by the group in this manner for very long. My competitive instincts simply wouldn't allow it. In fact, by November of that year I had already caught up with the group and was beating several of the girls regularly.

In these early days in Nottingham I was learning quickly, and part of the reason for this was my relationship with Head Coach Nick Gooch, which I have to say wasn't always easy or amenable in that first year.

In 2006, Nick – a former Olympic bronze medallist short track skater himself in the 1990s and the first Brit to win a short track Olympic medal of any colour – had just been promoted to Head Coach from Development Coach. At the same time, Stuart Horsepool had gone from Head Coach to Performance Director.

At that point, as much as we were told what to do, the hierarchical structure and the delineation of tasks within the programme was all a little disorganised and wishy-washy. Even I could see that, in these days pre-funding, there just wasn't enough expertise to go around.

Consequently, as much as you were clearly good enough to be on the programme in the first place, you weren't given total attention until you'd proved that you had the potential to become one of the very top athletes.

As much as Nick oversaw the whole team in theory, he

just couldn't be everything to all people, all of the time. As a rule the juniors definitely got less attention than seniors because of that. Sometimes, when we showed up in the mornings during that first season, there wouldn't be anyone available to coach us on the ice at all. Instead we'd just be thrown on a watt bike somewhere and told to train on our own.

That might sound easy and desirable but it really wasn't. I didn't want easy. I wanted to improve measurably with every single training session. To do that I needed someone physically there, spelling out goals in front of me in black and white. I needed someone to question – to *feed* off.

So at the start, given that I was one of these juniors, I had to impress Nick and fight for his attention. Obviously I wasn't the only one. It all became quite stressful to the extent that if you didn't have a competitive attitude, you didn't get noticed. And if you didn't get noticed, there was no way you could flourish. It really was a cut-throat culture back then. I knew that; everybody else knew it too. Inevitably, the strongest survived and others fell by the wayside. That was just how it was: the law of the jungle.

Nowadays elite sport coaching programmes are very different. Everything is much less dog-eat-dog. Athlete wellbeing, in theory at least, comes first, and that attitude extends to having two or three coaches in a programme to suit the various personality types within it.

Elite sport today is much more politically correct and inclusive than it was 15 years ago. Health and safety is paramount. While progress of this kind is undoubtedly a good thing, it certainly makes for an easier ride to the extent that I often laugh about it all with the young ones nowadays. "You have no idea how it was for us," I tell them. "You get everything on a plate."

In 2006, I had no problem with the 'one coach' approach in theory. The day-to-day siege mentality of a competitive environment where it was quite literally survival of the fittest actually played to my strengths.

Unfortunately, in practice it was more difficult, simply because I really didn't like Nick as a person. You'd never say that Nick is the most academic person on the planet in general terms. But in his specific area of expertise, short track speed skating, he has access to more knowledge than anyone I've ever met, and he has no problem letting you know it.

In all honesty, right from day one, I just thought he was a bit of an arrogant pain in the arse. I'm sure I didn't hide what I felt either!

In the years since, I've often thought about this schism we had between us at the beginning and I've come to the conclusion that it's easily explained: we're so similar as people. Nick and I are both very fact based. Mostly that was good; it meant we looked at things on the same plain. We're also extremely hot-headed and stubborn. That was not so good; neither of us would ever admit to being wrong when we clashed, as we frequently did.

However, the common trait that worked best was that

we were both, no matter what, totally motivated to do well and were emotionally invested in achieving real progress on a daily basis. That was like gold dust.

The way I see it, elite sport isn't a nine-to-five job, certainly not for an athlete like me. Every lap on the ice was maximal. I never once half-assed that last rep in the gym. Not once did I clock-watch. At no time was I on autopilot because I didn't feel like it that day.

Personally, I viewed every training session as if it was the most important thing in the world in that moment. And then, when I went home for the night after a long day, it wasn't as if I switched off – quite the opposite. As I'd done in my bedroom back in Livingston, I analysed everything I'd done that day to the finest detail. But instead of stewing over horrible comments from the girls at school, I analysed my training efforts and thought, *that's fine, but how do I go one better tomorrow?*

What's more, even as a 15-year-old, I expected the same level of dedication from my coach. Inevitably, not all are like that. But thank god Nick Gooch was. As long as he saw that you were putting in the effort, he'd go the extra mile with you. This attitudinal synergy between us was enough to eclipse any personality clashes we had.

What I found most interesting was that Nick wouldn't always focus his time on the most talented people.

Instead, he'd often give most to the people in the group who he saw to be trying the hardest and, most importantly, those that were actually listening to him and wanting to be better, as opposed to those that just got on the ice one day then didn't turn up for the next week because they had to be at college or something else. If you didn't bother, Nick didn't bother with you. I always respected that approach, even though some might consider that to be his main weakness. For me though, it worked.

In that respect at least, he and I were a very good match, to the extent that as much as Nick and I clashed on things all the time because of our similarities, he always went above and beyond as he could see I was willing to do anything possible to get better.

And in 2006, I definitely always was.

Let's just say that by the time I'd been in Nottingham for a few months and had been doing elite speed skating full time, I'd become insanely competitive with everybody, including myself and, for that matter, Nick.

At the same time, while I asked questions and really listened to everything Nick told me, I was also learning to be much more proactive than reactive. I wanted to train effectively; I wanted to push hard and beyond what was prescribed. As much as I didn't really like him, I still wanted to please him more than anything, no matter how much it physically hurt.

Looking back, I really pushed through the pain barrier in training in those first few months. And I did so because I was emotionally invested in it on a daily basis because I knew I'd be disappointed with myself if I didn't.

Pain, for an athlete, is an interesting concept. It's an

essential component of progress in a physical endeavour at the elite level. There's simply no way around it. We've all got to endure it somehow, but everyone processes it in a different way.

In my case, I could always take a lot of it but I've often wondered whether, generally, I have an unusually high pain threshold or whether it was my tolerance for discomfort that was higher than most other girls.

With hindsight I'm inclined to think it's both, and that allowed me to do more than others in pursuit of strength. Training is way more physically demanding than racing anyway. In a race, it's over so quickly. You don't have time to think about pain. But in training, it's relentlessly gruelling and agonising.

Consequently, I had to learn very early on that, when the legs are burning like never before, I had to take my mind elsewhere and think about some other mundane aspect of my day like, *did I lock the front door/turn the lights off when I left the house in the morning?*

Better still, beyond the physical pain, as I'd discovered when I first started speed skating a year earlier, I could use my sport as a means of combating emotional pain. Whenever I felt low, or insecure, I just trained harder. No matter what anyone ever said to me and no matter how much I reflected that negativity back on myself, skating could always make the pain and self-loathing go away.

Instinctively, I started using my talent for skating as a way of keeping myself sane and balanced from day to day.

Training was one thing; it made me feel good and kept me in routine. But if I won a race of any kind, my god I'd get an intoxicating high that would last for a couple of days whereby all the feelings of inadequacy would disappear.

For those blissful 48 hours, I'd actually like myself, the way I looked and the way I felt. Life became bearable. As fast as I might have been skating, until I physically crossed that winning line and received official confirmation that I was the best, I didn't even want to look in the mirror because I knew I'd find some fault with the person looking back.

It soon got to the point that, instead of being critical of my face, my legs or my ears, I was focusing all of my intention on being critical of my own skating instead. Believe me, if you're tuned in to your sport so acutely and so obsessively to the extent that your day-to-day self-worth depends on it, you can only get better. Even Nick has often said that the reason I'm so good is that I've always been so critical of myself. He knew that I knew that if I didn't deliver or put in the effort, I'd bloody hate myself afterwards. That's so true, and it's as primal a motivator as any athlete could want.

Nevertheless, it was as much of a surprise to me as everyone else in the group that I was selected for my first ever World Short Track Championships in Milan in March 2007, the first major competition of any note that I was eligible to compete at.

Historically, as I mentioned previously, the biggest problem with short track in the UK is that there really has never been much competitive racing available, certainly not for us girls. For a sport that's all about racing, that's a huge issue right off the bat. Of course, there were occasional invitational competitions that we could go to that were a level below European and World Cup level but beyond that there was nothing much unless you were up at the elite level.

So when it came to being selected for a major championships, yes I'd worked hard and had improved and sure I'd caught up on many of the others, but even I knew that I was by no means one of the best in real terms from a racing perspective – a fact that wasn't lost on some of the others in the group either.

"Why's she going and I'm not?" I'd hear people who weren't selected saying.

In a competitive programme like ours, jealousy of that kind was to be expected. In truth, I didn't really care what anyone said. The way I saw it, I was just pleasantly surprised to be included at all given that there hadn't been a lot to judge me on. As it happened, I went to Milan completely wide-eyed, competed and finished somewhere in the middle of the pack having raced in all three distances: 500m, 1000m and 1500m.

On one hand, I thought I did OK – and in my mind I certainly justified my selection to our team. Having said that, I do also clearly recall standing there at one point and thinking, *wow*....

Obviously, I had little by way of point of reference. I'd never been to a World Championship or a World Cup. I don't think I'd even seen either of them on TV. It was the first proper competition I'd ever been to in my life and I do remember watching some of these athletes and thinking, o*h my god, what am I doing? I'm rubbish...*

I was shocked at the gulf in standard. And really it should have come as no been no surprise when you consider that the difference between a British speed skater and the Canadian equivalent was that the Canadian, as I alluded to earlier, had probably been racing since they were three or four years old.

Meanwhile I'd been speed skating for a couple of years and only racing properly for a few months. Relatively speaking, as much as I'd been competing nationally, I felt that I didn't have a bloody clue what I was doing compared to these girls. As strong as I was (and I'd get much stronger), I knew I had so much to learn about racing.

I remember thinking to myself, *I'll probably never be a world champion...*

By any standards, it was a confusing end to my first season and as I usually did, in my mind I assessed where I'd got to from a tangible perspective. Everything always had to be measurable, and even I had to admit that I had made some strides.

At this point, a few months into the programme, we'd all been taught basically the same things: the correct skating technique and such like. And if we executed that technique to the letter, in theory we'd all be naturally more efficient on the ice.

But there's more to everything than just tangibles in

sport. Sometimes an athlete has a degree of X factor – an unidentifiable degree of extra ability that can't be easily explained but that elevates them above most others, and in a complex sport like short track where the body is everything, that's especially true.

For some reason that I can't explain, I've always had a very good awareness of my body and what it's doing at any given time.

Maybe it's because I was always so self-conscious about how I looked or felt when I was young. Or maybe it wasn't that at all – I don't really know.

Either way, as much as I didn't always get along with Nick, because of this innate understanding I had I was always able to talk to him and ask the kind of questions I needed to in order to figure out these subtle skating nuances. I always wanted to get better on my own, and he responded by helping me more.

Consequently, by the end of this first season, I'd arrived at an elevated, enlightened point where I really knew how to make my body incredibly efficient in terms of expending energy. In some ways that was a huge positive in that everything came so easily to me. On the ice, I didn't really have to try too hard to be good.

But the flipside was that because it was all so easy, I'd get lazy and almost sleepy, as if I was in some kind of trance, to the extent that I'd find myself talking to myself saying things like, *Elise you need to move your legs more*, even if I didn't really need to. Whenever I watched a video of myself skating, it always looked like I wasn't doing much and I used to think, *that looks piss easy!*

Again, I have no idea how I was able to understand all this at such a young age. And if I ever become a coach, I'm not sure whether I'd be able to explain it all to someone else in a way that would make any sense.

Because I'm better at articulating myself now than when I was 15, I can occasionally get through to someone nowadays who needs help with a particular aspect of skating that's a bit more subtle – like feel or how to conserve energy efficiently while still moving fast.

Back then there was no chance. As much as I knew about how skating should feel, there was no way in hell I could relay that to anyone else. Take Charlotte for example. In some ways she had so many qualities I didn't have. On a watt bike – a key part of off-ice training – she was way better than I ever was.

Equally, I'm sure she'd concede that, towards the end of that first season, I was the better skater between us. I knew what I did that she didn't that made me better. Every time she skated it was obvious to me. But could I articulate that to her in a way she could understand and then implement it? Could I hell! I could explain the principles of technique to her, but that didn't necessarily translate into her skating any easier.

THREE

PROVE IT

BY THE END OF THAT FIRST SEASON AND towards the beginning of the second, my relationship with Nick improved only marginally, largely due to the fact that it was becoming apparent to everyone, including him, that I had the potential to be very good.

By the autumn of 2007, in my mind I was already very good within the context of my peer group in Nottingham, but at that point Nick was still very focused on Sarah Lindsay, who was considered to be the prize asset of the team, probably because she was the oldest and most experienced (and that they'd dated previously). Theirs was a completely different kind of relationship.

By this point, I saw myself as a sprinter, and over 500m (the shortest competition distance) I knew I was already faster than Sarah and trained harder. The problem was that, at World Cup events, when you had two athletes, the coach had to split them between the distances and Sarah always got the 500m and I didn't

Annoyingly, the reason for this wasn't always based on who was the best. In those days, there was definitely an age and experience-based hierarchy in British sport that never made any sense to me. I thought it was all absolute bollocks.

But as much as I felt that way, I always did as I was told, unlike youngsters now. Jeez, if I had spoken to my elders back in 2007 like the kids speak to me nowadays, I'd have got my arse kicked I can promise you that!

But that's just how sport was back then. It was a different world and as much as I moaned, threw my helmet around a bit and cried at various times about what I saw as injustices, I still just got on with it. Every time I was faced with any kind of setback, I'd just say, over and over again, *I'm going to prove it. I'll just have to prove it…*

As much as I was competing with Sarah, who is now one of my closest friends, back in the day she was simultaneously a big sister figure and someone who was willing to be quite hard on me, especially given that she could clearly see that I was coming up the rankings and beating her.

I can't blame her for feeling that way at all. If someone did that to me, I'd be pretty annoyed too, and I don't mind admitting that I have been a bit harsh on youngsters myself in recent years. I think it's a natural response if you're a competitive person. You're simply marking your territory.

Occasional hard-edged comments aside, I couldn't have survived the first few years in Nottingham without Sarah.

She taught me to cook, to clean and how to live like a professional athlete. I really missed her when she left the team after the Olympics in Vancouver in 2010 and we're still super-close friends now.

Throughout the 2007/2008 and 2008/2009 seasons I honed my craft and did so on the back of skating in as many competitions as were available to me. In addition to the six World Cup events that take place each year: four before Christmas and two afterwards, I also skated at European Championships, Invitational Cups, Star Classes, UK National Championships, World Junior Championships and British Open Championships.

From memory, and my recollection is a little hazy given how often I competed during these early years, my first major final outside of National competitions was at a World Cup event in Dresden in February 2009, where I came second in a 1500m race behind Germany's Christin Priebst.

In January 2010, I reached a major milestone when I medalled for the first time in my career at the European Championships in Dresden, finishing in second place behind Arianna Fontana of Italy in 1500m.

At the time, I was actually shocked to medal at all. As much as Nick had always told me I would medal, I don't think I ever really felt that it would happen. I just didn't think I was that good at that time relative to the other girls on the circuit.

But in actual fact, I was considerably better than I

thought. Looking back on that 1500m race, I know now that I might well have won it if I had just stayed calm.

In a slow race, I sat in fifth until we had just under three laps to go, then I made what was a pretty bold move around the outside and found myself sitting right on Arianna's shoulder with one lap to go. I could have gone past, but at the time I didn't, but only because I couldn't quite believe that I'd got there. That moment of hesitation cost me a first gold medal. I didn't quite have the speed to pick her up before the line.

The Vancouver Olympics in February 2010 for me was a massive watershed in so many ways.

On one hand I'd improved out of sight as a skater and was becoming a more rounded person as I became accustomed to the athlete life. On the other, while Sarah was definitely still the focus, Nick was certainly keeping an eye on me more and more, presumably because, seeing as Vancouver was going to be her last Olympics, he saw me as Sarah's natural successor given that I'd shown that I could handle the big stage at the Europeans a few weeks prior.

As an overall experience, Vancouver was definitely my favourite Olympics, and that wasn't just because it was my first.

As a team, as much as we had both Team GB rules and our own rules within the short track team to abide by every day, things were pretty laid back out in Canada because of the general environment we were in. As long as we always signed out and signed into the athlete village and didn't take the piss, we were all allowed to go down town into Vancouver, which is obviously a great city, whenever we wanted.

Everything was so accessible, everyone was very friendly and the stadiums were always full. Having never been to North America before, I loved every second of those 2010 Winter Olympics.

On the ice, again I did OK but no better than that – finishing 11th, 19th and 20th in the 500m, 1000m and 1500m events respectively. It hadn't been a disaster, but when I left Vancouver I couldn't help feeling a bit empty and defeated.

As I thought about everything on the flight back, for the first time, at the age of 19, I started wondering about what the hell I was doing with my life.

The way I saw it, given where I'd finished in all three competitive distances, I was miles away from winning an Olympic medal. Even on paper, this was indisputable. In 11th, 19th and 20th positions, it wasn't as if I was close or had been unlucky. There were a lot of girls between the three medal positions and me.

My biggest concern was that I couldn't immediately think how I could conceivably bridge that gap. In fact, if you'd asked me straight after Vancouver if I thought I'd ever win an Olympic medal of any colour in my career, I'd have said there was no chance whatsoever.

Why was that, you might ask?

Well, as much as I'd got to where I had through sheer hard work, pro-activity and a degree of natural ability, I just didn't think that, as a country, we had either the plan or the resources in place to win short track medals at major championships.

Let's be honest, in 2010, Britain wasn't doing very well in any sports. I didn't want to chase something that, as a country and a system, we were simply not very good at. On that basis, it didn't matter how good I was if the culture I came from continually held me back.

All of this might sound as if I was being a bit negative, defeatist and entitled given I was just a kid and it was only my first Olympics. But from my perspective, I really didn't have any interest whatsoever in going through all the training I was enduring and getting paid next to nothing for doing so, if there was no possibility of ever winning a medal at the end of it. I wasn't interested in just 'doing well' in the sport.

I didn't want to be one of those typically British gallant losers.

As harsh an assessment as this might sound, I thought, *why are we even doing this?*

As much as I knew that getting to an Olympic Games at all is something that most people never do, I had no desire to do it all again just to say I'd been at another one. At the same time I also knew that, if I didn't commit to skating, the only alternative was probably going to be to quit, go home to Scotland and start a different life while I still could – and maybe become the aircraft engineer I'd always fancied being.

When I got back from Vancouver, I met with Nick almost immediately.

"There's no point in carrying on with this if I'm just going to do the same thing all over again," I told him.

"So what do you want to do?" he asked.

I made the decision right there and then. And it wasn't to go back to Livingston to become an aircraft engineer.

"I want to become the best. I want to win Olympic medals," I told him, staring across the table.

I should say at this point that at no point did I think I couldn't become the best. But what I did know was that I certainly couldn't do it all on my own, as much as people might have given me vague, "You can do it!" type of encouragement.

Platitudes like that have never registered with me. I don't want to hear them; I'll have them picked apart and discarded in my head as quickly as anyone can say the words. For example, if you were to say to me, "Oh you've done this, therefore you should probably be able to do that" I would just think, *you don't really know that for sure.*

However, if you're logical with me you can keep me out of the emotional/irrational zone that I can definitely fall into. Essentially, I always need hard evidence.

Equally, what I needed from 2010 onwards was organised, systematic support from a team. I also wanted logical, identifiable series of goals and milestones that I could achieve and check-off as I went.

Again, for me, unless something could be measured and

therefore become indisputable, it simply did not exist.

"OK, how do we do it all?" Nick said.

"We put a four-year plan in place," I told him.

What I told him was half right, but what it actually became was an eight-year plan that would take me to the 2014 Olympics in Sochi, and then onwards to the 2018 Olympics in PyeongChang.

Looking back, it was a huge turning point, not just for me but I also think it created a bit of a precedent for British sport thereafter.

Many meetings followed, where I had to sit down and be part of a large team who, between us, put all these goals and plans on paper in a way that I could see happening.

Again, as much as I'm driven by emotions a lot of the time, facts and actualities drive me more. It was no good me saying, "I'm going to find a way to become the best" unless I could actually see, before my own eyes, on paper, what I and we needed to do to make it all happen.

And we got there.

This plan was fluid and came with clearly defined goals: by X date I'll have medalled at a World Championship. And if that happens, by Y date I'll win European gold. If I stick to the training schedule Z, and so on, then I'd go on to win a World Championship, and then an Olympic medal. To get to these checkpoints, my training plan was detailed and specifically focused on my strengths and weaknesses.

One such weakness was the shortcoming I first identified in Milan in 2007: I simply didn't have the racing experience these other girls had. I was still learning – I still am today. As much as I could improve that side of my skating – with more racing, to a small degree – I knew that alone probably wasn't going to be enough and it became clear that refining other areas of my skating would become crucial.

That acknowledgment, in March 2010, that my relative lack of racing experience was and would always be my weakness was a highly significant one. On one hand it was certainly a little depressing to realise that the short track culture in the UK was holding me back. But at the same time I found myself thinking, *so what do I have over these girls?*

I had no interest in meekly accepting that they had an advantage and simply saying, *that's just how it is.* That would have been a typically British thing to do. Instead, I wanted to counteract it, and to do so I had to be proactive.

The first attribute of mine was that I was certain I had a willingness/ability to train harder than any other girl and I reasoned that if I trained harder, I would therefore be indisputably stronger. And from there I arrived at a place where I truly believed that if I became stronger, then I couldn't possibly be beaten.

Next I reflected on the fact that a lot of the other top girls were quite a lot taller than me. To that end, I deduced that my power-to-weight ratio, given that I am quite petite, could be another major edge. I thought, *well, I will just improve that power-to-weight ratio even further...*

As I formulated all of the details that helped create the

training goal angle of this eight-year plan, I could feel my mindset changing.

From a place where I'd been watching these girls thinking, *how do I beat them?* I flipped it all around totally to where the more pertinent question became, having negated any of their advantages in my mind, *how do I make them have to beat me?*

It was so huge to shift focus by acknowledging this and to have this plan in hand with every checkpoint plotted and the actions required to arrive at each spelled out in a way that was so clear and so based on cast-iron facts.

Obviously, there had to be some scope to revise things if something unexpected happened or a goal changed, but fundamentally I could see what I had to do and I believed in it totally.

By the end of these meetings, in my head I knew I could be the best short track skater in the world, simply because there were no reasons left to make me think that I couldn't.

Everything on the plan from my personal end was doable and my belief was reinforced further by the fact I had an answer to every other kind of problem – many of which were just bureaucratic issues anyway – that all the various team members came up with during the conversations:

"Well, we don't get as much ice time as everyone else."

"We don't race train like everyone else."

"Yeah, but we just don't have the facilities that other teams have."

"Well, we don't have the money that everyone else has."

There was all of that, and probably a few more excuses that I can't remember. It's so funny to think back on all of this now – especially given that, here I am, 30 years old and I still have made absolutely no money ever out of this sport.

At the time I just sat there calmly, as the excuses rained in, and said, "Well, I can see an answer to every one of these problems that you're talking about".

If we didn't have as much ice time, I'd do even more off the ice.

If I didn't race as much, I'd just have to be so strong that it wouldn't matter.

Need more money? Find it from somewhere…

I had solutions to everything, and at the end of it I just sat there calm as you like and said, "Yeah, I'm doing this".

And as I said it, it was as if I could see Nick Gooch's face forgetting all about Sarah Lindsay and buying into our vision, right before my eyes. It was a significant turning point in our athlete/coach relationship.

It had taken me three years, but I'd earned his respect at what was undoubtedly the tipping point of my entire short track career.

Sarah Lindsay retired after the Vancouver Olympics having been the British Ladies Champion for nine years running. But in three attempts she never made an Olympic final in any distance, far less medalled.

That wasn't necessarily her fault, either. Sarah was a talented, dedicated skater and the best Britain had for a long time. But she was unfortunate to have competed in an era of British sport where there was little or no help from the culture

By the early summer of 2010, I'd long moved out of the figure skating coach's house and had a place of my own. In between, I'd stayed at Charlotte's place in town for a few months, as her dad had recently moved down to Nottingham to live.

The financial side of being an athlete in a relatively minority sport like short track was never easy. For the first year, I didn't get paid at all so my mum covered all of my expenses because she wanted me to focus on my training and to not have to also get a job. In the second year, I started getting paid £140 per month in addition to another £300 that I never actually saw and which went to cover my accommodation.

There was never much spare money around, and as you might imagine, many of my thoughts around the time, when I became old enough to get one at all, were centred around the mindset of, *I need to get as many overdrafts as possible!* One of them still isn't totally paid off even today.

As much of a plate-spinning exercise as my finances were (and largely still are), at no point did I ever consider quitting because of a lack of money. In fact, one of the things that always grates with me nowadays is when I hear athletes in my sport or similar minority sports saying, when they're funding is taken away: "Oh, well I can't do what I want to do because I've not got any money."

Let's be honest, with UK Sport, it's made pretty clear

to athletes what needs to be done to secure funding. You've got to prove that you're good to even get money for a start. Equally, it's abundantly clear that there is never going to be enough money to go around for every athlete in every sport. That's just how the lottery funding system works. It's not perfect, but it's better than nothing.

Don't get me wrong. I'm not saying it's going to be easy if you're not a funded athlete. I would have hated to not be funded during the earlier part of my career. But if I hadn't been, I promise you it wouldn't have altered my attitude one bit.

The reason for that is that I knew I was going into a niche sport at the outset. I willingly went into a sport I knew wasn't very well funded, didn't attract lucrative sponsors and didn't pay particularly well – certainly not as well as being a track and field athlete for example.

But I chose to do this, and in doing so I made a promise to myself that I'd always stand by that decision no matter how bad the finances were. The way I saw it, what I was doing was an absolute privilege anyway but just because I was doing it didn't mean I should automatically be paid for it.

The same applies to every athlete starting out. In other jobs you don't necessarily get the best pay when you first start out in a first job. Sometimes people even have to work for free to begin with. But pursuing elite sport isn't even the same as getting a job in my opinion. I think you've only really got the job when you're truly good at that sport. I

elt at home on the ice straightaway but I also swapped figure skating for speed skating as soon as I could!

Growing up in Livingst
with mum Angela and
brother Jamie, was not
always easy but the love
we had for each other w
always there. The pictur
below is that of a typical
adolescent, trying to fin
a way to combine speed
skating with having a
teenage social life!

Training at the Agora ice rink in
Milan prior to the World Short Track
Speed Skating Championship,
held there in March 2007

Getting ready to race at the British Short Track Championships at the National Ice Centre in Nottingham – a place that has played a huge part in my development

I could get used to this! I celebrate winning the Junior Women's title alongside Mohawks' Charlotte Gilmartin (left) and Aldwych's Helen Clark at the British Short Track Championships in March 2009

Sarah Lindsay and I unveil the 2010 Winter Olympics kit during a photocall at Somerset House, London, in January 2010. These kinds of events come as part of the job and I am now far more comfortable than I used to be in front of the camera

Not a bad view for a bike ride, even if I didn't go anywhere! Here I am staying active in the British base at the 2010 Winter Olympics in Vancouver

Preparing for the challenge of winning the Short Track 1000m in Vancouver. The thrill of competing at an Olympics is indescribable and I consider myself very lucky to have represented Team GB at three Games

If ever two pictures could highlight the peaks and the troughs of competition then these are surely it. On the left I am ecstatic at having come through my Short Track 500m heat but the disappointment is there for all to see as I then failed to qualify for the semi-final

Myself and Alex Stanley sharing a laugh in training back at the National Ice Centre in Nottingham

Showing off the tools of my trade

The fastest six Brits on skates meet up for a Team GB photoshoot. I'm pictured here with, left to right, Charlotte Gilmartin, Richard Shoebridge, Jon Eley, Paul Stanley and Ian Upcott

On my way to winning the women's 1500m final at the Short Track Speed Skating World Cup in Dresden, Germany, in February 2013

know a lot of people won't like that opinion but that's how
I feel

Anyway...

By 2010, things had changed a little for the better on the
financial front. By finishing in second place in the 1000m
(and third place overall) at that European Championships
in Dresden in January, prior to the Vancouver Olympics the
following month, I qualified for what is known as 'B Card'
for the season that followed, 2010/2011, beginning in April
of that year.

In material terms, that took my earnings from about
£500 per month up to about £1700. By my measurement, I'd
got the job, albeit the 'A card' was another level of funding
above that, and to achieve that I needed a top three finish
at either a Worlds or an Olympic Games.

This, obviously, was a welcome wage rise. I could just
about live on that. But what was less welcome was the fact
that it felt to me as if UK Sport did everything in their
power at the time to stop me getting it!

For whatever reason, it was always a whole lot of aggro
trying to get money out of them and the impression I got
was that they just thought we were stupid teenagers who'd
just end up spending money on pointless things.

But the reality was that by that point I had my own
place, a mortgage and was struggling to keep up with the
pressure. I *needed* that money, and not for Botox injections
or eyelash extensions.

Where else was I going to get it? I didn't want to bother

my mum about it; she'd helped me enough, but it was annoying that we always seemed to have to fight to get paid in the first place, and then for the amount to be actually right each month.

Irritations with UK Sport's payment habits aside, I was at least independent by March 2010 in the sense that I'd just moved into my own place and while my personal life wasn't what you'd call perfect (I'd just split up with my first proper boyfriend) things were at least stable. Of course, I also now had the eight-year plan in place to keep me goal-focused and in routine.

As independent as I was, I was still relatively naive in a variety of ways. For example, by the time I was 19, I had only ever had one drink in my life – on the night of my 18th birthday. Drinking and smoking had been totally off limits when I was young. My mother would have absolutely kicked my butt if I'd tried any such thing at 15. Then I went to the Olympics in Vancouver and when everything finished we all got drunk. That was the sum extent of my drinking exploits to that point.

However, something then happened to me out on the town that underlined just why going out and drinking had never been my idea of fun.

FOUR

RAPE

AFTER I GOT BACK FROM THE WORLD
Championships in Sofia in March 2010, where I came a
distant fourth in the 1000m final, I went out for a couple
of drinks in Nottingham city centre because it was now the
off-season.

In four years it was the only time I'd gone on a proper
night out. As I said, I was no drinker at that time. I
consciously avoided drinking and anytime I did it was
always lightweight alcopop stuff. If I had a couple of glasses
of proper wine I'd probably have fallen to bits.

I remember going into this bar in town; I was with a
teammate at the time. We bought a drink and I had only
got through a couple of sips when this guy came over to
me and started talking. I was just chatting back without
thinking about it too much. Again, I was quite naïve and
not at all used to those kinds of social situations.

Then he offered to get me a drink, whereupon I told him that I already had a drink – a drink that I'd barely touched. But he went and got one anyway and came back with it saying, "Try this one".

I had a couple of sips of this new drink. Again, I was too naïve to know any better. Even then I still hadn't had an entire drink in total, but I remember saying to myself, *man, I'm really fucked.*

At the time I had no idea what was happening and by this point my teammate had gone off with some other guy. I looked around and also remember thinking to myself, *I'm not staying out feeling like this. This is not good.*

It wasn't even late anyway. It must have been ten o'clock.

I walked out of the bar into the street, and in those days before Uber, I called for a taxi and waited. Meanwhile, this guy from the bar appeared out of nowhere. The taxi was nowhere in sight.

I can't remember exactly what happened next and in what order. I was strangely impaired and my body wasn't functioning properly at all. I tried to run away from him but I simply couldn't run.

I was falling on the ground after every other step. Even in situations when I've been absolutely wasted since, I've never felt like I did that night.

As hard as I tried, I just couldn't get away from this guy. Whenever I fell on the floor, he kept running after me, picking me up and dragging me, eventually into the taxi, which by this time had appeared at the side of the road.

I don't recall much about the taxi journey, but I do remember – through the brain fog and fractured memories – saying to the taxi driver: "Please don't take me to this guy's house. You've got to take me home."

At one point, we actually drove quite close to where I lived and by this point I was fucking screaming, "There! We need to turn down there!"

Meanwhile this guy was laughing and clearly trying to play the whole situation down so as not to make the taxi driver suspicious, saying, "She's my girlfriend. She's drunk. She doesn't know what she's on about, mate".

Basically, at the end of this taxi journey this guy took me into his house. It was clear to me right then that he was going to sexually assault me and the whole time I was repeatedly telling him, "No. No".

At that point in my life I'd only ever had sex with one boy. He was a longish-term boyfriend and we'd only recently broken up. Whenever we'd had sex he'd always used a johnnie. Regardless, as much as I was saying no, this guy kept forcing himself onto me, and, ultimately *into* me, without protection.

Now, I'm feisty and strong and could probably push most lads off me if I had to on my best day. But in this state I just couldn't fight this guy off at all. As hard as I tried, my arms were flopping. I could wriggle, but I just couldn't get up. In the end I just gave in and let it happen. At some point I must have passed out. When I woke up in the middle of the night, I was reminded in gross, graphic terms what had happened earlier. I stood up, grabbed my stuff and legged it out of the place.

In the days immediately afterwards I didn't go to the police to report it.

I *never* went to the police to report it.

In fact, as I sit and write this book, only four people in my life know about what happened that night, and one of them is the doctor I went to see to get checked over and to make sure I'd hadn't got fucking AIDS or some other kind of sexually transmitted disease that would ruin my life.

I was so naïve about all of that stuff as it was. If I had picked up a disease, I'd have probably blamed myself.

Now, I know some people reading this will think, "Why didn't you report it or tell someone in authority?" and that's a valid question.

But at the time I just didn't know what to do. I definitely didn't want to tell my mum because I knew that it would only upset her. From a team perspective there was nobody in an official capacity there to offer any kind of pastoral support. I certainly couldn't have talked to Nick about it in 2010. We just didn't have the relationship that we developed in later years at that time.

Truthfully, I didn't even want to tell anyone.

I just wanted to black it all out until the right opportunity came along to tell the story, and this book seemed like the logical time and place to put what happened that night into some kind of context.

I was young and so inexperienced, and I just didn't have

anyone around me that I trusted enough to tell. Furthermore, in the days immediately after the rape I went up to Scotland for a few weeks before the new season started.

While I was up there, I was in absolute turmoil. I was withdrawn and anxious to the point that I'm sure my mother wondered what the hell was going on. But by the time I returned to England it felt like I'd already gone past that logical window where it's considered reasonable to report a serious sexual assault.

The other thought on my mind was whether anyone would even believe me if I did report it anyway. We've all seen the stories and the resulting opinions that people put forward in these instances; stuff about his word again mine or a lack of evidence or that "She was asking for it".

Don't get me wrong. I'm no hardline feminist. I have read about situations where a woman has been sexually assaulted and when I process the precise circumstances even I have found myself thinking, *you might just have put yourself in that situation there…*

Because of all the above, for a while, I even started convincing myself that it was actually my fault for going out in town in the first place. But then I rationalised everything and reassured myself that nothing had happened that I could be blamed for.

In fact, having been quite drunk several times since this assault, I know beyond question that what happened that night was something completely else altogether. I wasn't just pissed. My body, which I've always known and understood well, was totally incapacitated by what must have been some kind of date rape drug.

As much as I might have occasionally, in weak, misplaced guilt-ridden moments, blamed myself for having a drink at all, deep down I knew that I'd barely had a drink and that none of what happened was my fault in any way. I wasn't 'asking for it'. I wasn't looking for anything at all. I just went out, got drugged and then got raped by some random lad against my will. That's the long and short of it.

Looking back now through more experienced eyes, I also think I had a fundamentally different view of what rape was back in 2010.

I initially thought, *well, I can't really say I've been raped because I haven't been beaten up.*

I always thought that rape was what you saw on TV shows – where someone gets grabbed in a park, dragged into the bushes, battered, raped and left for dead. That hadn't happened to me. I wasn't punched or beaten and I wasn't left out in the cold. But I *was* forced to have sex against my will and at the time I just wasn't mature enough to know that the two are exactly the same.

It was a year until I told anyone at all about that night I was raped.

And the reason for that was that I actually felt ashamed – which I now know is completely the wrong way to feel about this. I had no reason to apologise for anything although, bizarrely, the guy in question felt the need to apologise to me on bloody Facebook.

Somehow he found me. In those days before there were more thorough privacy options, it was so much easier to find people. He could have easily done so by searching 'Elise' and gone from there. He started sending me direct messages, apologising. I didn't respond to any of them.

I only ever knew his name because of his Facebook profile.

The next off-season, when I was on a night out with Charlotte, we walked past the guy in the street. When I saw his face, I had a panic attack on the spot.

Charlotte couldn't understand what was going on so I had to tell her the basics of the story. In a year, she was the first person I ever told, and I think I only did so because I had to.

There was no other way to explain the visceral reaction I had when I saw the guy's face again. Seeing it took me right back to that night, with him looming above me, pinning my impaired body to the floor in a strange house.

Even with her, for some reason I didn't feel the need to go into drastic detail. I just said something like: "I had a bad experience with him once."

"What do you mean?" she said.

As much of a gross understatement as my explanation was, I just didn't want to go into it. As much as Charlotte was my best friend, I'd only really known her for two years. I wasn't comfortable revisiting it and, in retrospect, I think that's because I did feel a little abandoned in Nottingham in those early years.

With hindsight, as much as I thank my mother for shielding me from everything that's bad in the world for the first years of my life, it did mean that I was a little underprepared for dealing with something as awful as being raped, not that anyone ever is.

Predictably, I'm still dealing with the consequences of that night. A few things in life have negatively affected me but I think the rape, and the timing of it, affected me more than anything.

I'd just come back from my first Olympic Games and having done all the work with the team to create a plan, finally it felt like I had a clearly defined purpose in life that was helping me build my self-esteem and overcome my insecurities.

However, for that to then happen to me when I had no support network around me was devastating and it undoubtedly changed my worldview and set me back so much.

More than anything, it fundamentally changed the way I interact with men. Even before the rape, I was never the kind of girl who could even consider a one-night stand. For me, it has always taken a lot for me to become comfortable with the opposite sex and get at all close. I'm not naturally touchy-feely at all. I'd never even kissed a boy until I was 17.

Being raped really put me off even talking to people on a night out. Nowadays I don't even look people in the eye. I shouldn't have to feel like that.

RAPE

Why the fuck should I hide away?

Instead, the guy who did this to me should be in jail. But hey, it's too late, I guess. I should have been braver at the time.

FIVE

UP IN FLAMES

AS TRAUMATISED AS I WAS, AND STILL AM, BY the events of that night in 2010, it wasn't long until my life added another layer of trauma for me to deal with.

By this point, as I said, I had my own apartment and as much as I enjoyed having it, the interest-only mortgage I'd taken out after buying the place with some money I'd been left was stretching my modest financial resources to absolute breaking point.

That said, I loved the place and it felt like, for the first time, I had a home where I could come and go at will and by that time I was also dating my first serious boyfriend, Jack Whelbourne, who was also a skater on the national team programme. All was pretty good in my world.

However, one night, in June 2012, everything changed.

As I was lying asleep in bed in the middle of the night, Jack woke me up because of the dense, choking black smoke that was filling the rest of the flat. I hadn't been aware of any of it; no smoke detectors had been triggered at all. Had he not woken me up, I'd still be sleeping now.

My first thought wasn't for me, or for that matter, Jack. It was for the two cats I had by that time. I quickly found one of them, and it was safe. Unable to find the other, I was panicking, totally unsure what to do and when. I was sure I was going to die that night.

Meanwhile, Jack had phoned the fire brigade and it seemed like no time at all until they were outside, sirens wailing, lights flashing, shouting at us through the window.

"Leave everything. You've got to get out now," they told me.

I was only wearing a pair of baggy shorts and a top at the time but what else could I do but climb out of the window into the night air? All I remember is sitting in the ambulance saying, "I'm not leaving without my cat. You have to go back for my cat".

"We need to get you to hospital. You have smoke inhalation," they told me.

"Not until you find my cat," I said.

After a few minutes of looking around, they came back and told me that they'd found the cat, and so off we went. I didn't know at the time if that was the truth or not, but in the long run the cat was outside the apartment when I eventually went back a day later. It had never been outside before so I'm glad it didn't do a runner.

Anyway, everything after them telling me they'd found

the cat was a complete daze. As I sat in the resuscitation room at the hospital, unaware that my hair and face were completely blackened by smoke, I felt like the only survivor in one of those zombie holocaust movies. I had nothing. No phone, no belongings and no money.

I don't even remember how and when I went back to the burnt-out flat, which by that time had that horrendous post-fire smell and was soaking wet.

When I walked in the door, I couldn't believe how bad it looked and I couldn't comprehend that I'd managed to get out alive. The only saving grace was that, because there were fire doors installed in the apartment, one room was completely untouched. For the next few months, while everything was fixed and cleaned, I stayed with Charlotte.

As I said, this fire, on top of everything else that had happened, damaged me. Not only did it upset the basic level of security I'd worked so hard to create for myself since arriving in a new city at the age of 15, but it also did so much emotional damage to what was already a confused, fragile 22-year-old girl who perpetually seemed to be dangling on the edge of one abyss or another.

However, I'm nothing if not strong and resilient.

No matter what happens to me, while I might bend and falter at times and completely lose my shit, I will not break. I have no idea where that strength comes from, but every time I'm in trouble or at what many might see as an absolutely irretrievable breaking point, I always find a way to dig in, look for a positive to cling on to and keep going.

The only thing that could possibly keep me going in 2012 was my skating. The plan that would hopefully get me to what could be seen as the promised land a year and a half down the line – the Olympic Games in Sochi in February 2014 – became more important than ever.

As an overall experience, Sochi was far better than I expected given the negative build-up the games got in the press. The BOA were really good there and the villages were all quite close together, which in turn meant that we could at least mix with some of the snowboarders and other teams in the British contingent.

On reflection, my experiences in Vancouver in 2010, where we were close to town and could come and go as we pleased, probably spoiled me a little. Sochi wasn't really like that; you pretty much had to stay inside the athlete village for the duration of the games.

Even if you did go out, because the security was so tight, it would take you half an hour to leave and another half an hour on your return. Then everyone's accreditation passes kept breaking, which just added more time. It just wasn't worth the aggravation to leave.

It wasn't as if there was anything to do on the outside anyway. Unlike Vancouver, where there were streets and shops to wander around, if you wanted to get anywhere from Sochi, you had to get on a train and travel for a minimum of half an hour. There just wasn't anything around and, in truth, things weren't that welcoming.

Unlike Vancouver, where people were friendly enough in

and around the stadiums themselves, in Russia, people were less forthcoming and the stadiums were rarely full anyway. As good as it all might have looked on TV, there was no colour and vibrancy in Sochi. Everything was painted white and the infrastructure felt quite sterile and incomplete – to the extent that it felt like they were still building things around us when we were there.

We never had any problems per se, but I heard various stories about toilet doors breaking and people getting locked inside. A gym hadn't been finished on time and therefore had to be re-situated into a tent. For a major international sporting event there was definitely a hint of work-in-progress about everything.

However, the most eye-opening aspect of the Sochi Olympics in 2014 was the doping protocols. Everything was slightly different. To me, that seemed just a touch suspicious.

Olympic protocols in general are different from other championships. In short track, obviously we operate under standard WADA rules like everyone else: where you have to be at a certain place at a specific hour of the day and such like.

In addition, at normal championships, they normally pull two to three skaters from each race. First place always gets checked, and then the others would be at random. Also, obviously, if a world record gets broken, that would be checked too. But no matter where you finish, you always have to stay until the end of the day just in case.

At the Olympics, they follow the same procedure within the competition, but in addition, they can also turn up at random in the village, no matter the time of day. You could have literally just got back from training and be lying down in your apartment for a rest, and someone could turn up at your door saying, "Doping!"

Mostly it's urine samples they take, but at the Olympics you can get both urine and blood taken. Sometimes they come around loads, which is obviously great for the integrity of the sport, but it can get to a point where you're thinking, *come on, give me a break!*

At Sochi, however, there were a few procedures that seemed weird. The main was related to the barcodes you are given to stick onto your sample. Normally, the other part of that barcode would be ripped off and given to the athlete in the event that there's an issue and the two barcodes need to be matched up later. In that sense, one part is as important as the other to prevent samples getting lost or mixed up.

Well, in Sochi they didn't ever give us our half of the barcode; they took it away instead. When that first happened, I thought, *hmmm, interesting.*

I just thought it was a bit suspicious at the time and I remember getting into a long argument with one of the doping officers about it all and I think we ended up reaching a compromise whereby he wrote details of our conversation down at the bottom of the form in the event that something did go wrong.

To me it was all a bit dodgy, and when it came out later

that Russia had been doing what they were doing, it all made sense.

Although it's obviously just me speculating here, but why else would they keep the duplicate barcodes if it wasn't for the purposes of swapping Russian athletes' dirty samples for other clean ones by using these barcode counterfoils? Why else wouldn't they give us our barcodes back? We might never really know, but that's certainly how it looks to me.

While Vancouver had been my baptism as an up-and-coming junior member of the team, you could say that Sochi in 2014 was the first Olympics I went to where – although it wasn't the specific goal as per the eight-year plan – I nevertheless had a realistic chance to win a medal if all the cards fell my way. While I wasn't experienced at being at the top, the capability was definitely there. By 2014 I was just about finding a way to mix it with the top girls.

Even then, you couldn't exactly say that I'd been a prolific winner in the lead-in. I had only consistently started to medal in that 2013/2014 season (Bronze at the World Championships in Hungary and two gold medals at the European Championships in Malmo). By winning bronze at the World Championships, I moved up to the top level of UK Sport funding – 'A Card' – from the beginning of the 2013/2014 season and although I wasn't living in luxury, life became just that little more manageable.

In every sense I was progressing steadily and it felt good that because I'd won those medals, and apparently had a bit of a personality, I was starting to get a few hundred followers on social media who all thought that I was amazing. For someone who'd never had any acceptance before and for whom the only means of feeling any self-worth at all was from skating, I can't even tell you how great that felt, even with the relatively low level profile I had.

Another massive positive was that, despite some of the emotional turmoil of the previous four years, I went into Sochi 100 per cent physically fit. I might not have been the fastest going into the competition, but I was certainly the strongest.

By this point I was pretty clear in my head that 500m was the distance I had potential to be the best at. I was fast enough and I was unbelievably strong, so in my mind I was sure that if I got out in front in the 500m, nobody was going to be able to get past me. I reckoned I'd be unbeatable.

In a 500m race, if you're drawn in Lane 1 or Lane 2 and you're one of the better skaters off the start, you've got a serious chance of winning. For me, I always felt that if I got to the first block in the lead in a 500m race, I'd almost certainly win unless someone knocked me over.

I didn't even necessarily see outside lines as being prohibitive. No matter what happens, you're unlikely to ever get a chance to nick up the inside in a top level 500m race anyway. Everyone will be blocking; there will never be a truly clear passage.

The only way to pass is around the outside, and to make a serious move around the outside, you're going to have to expend a lot of energy at some stage of the race.

In my opinion, this was where my strength could be my trump card in the sense that, even if I did have an outside draw and therefore had to go further to win, I could do it because in my opinion I was so much stronger than everyone else.

Nick disagreed about pretty much all of this! He thought my best distance was the 1500m, to the extent that it was a bit of an ongoing bone of contention between us. The two distances are so fundamentally different.

While 1500m might be considered a middle distance on an athletics track, in the context of our sport it is undoubtedly an endurance event whereas the 500m is just a straight, take-no-prisoners sprint. The 1000m, obviously, sits in the middle and is a subtle blend of speed and endurance.

From a physical perspective, Nick's opinion held some water I suppose. Because I was so strong, you could argue that on paper an endurance discipline did play to my strengths somewhat. But from a tactical perspective I never really felt I was skilled enough or calm enough to win 1500m races at the top level.

In a 1000m race you want to fight to get to the front and hope you can hold on. I had the power/endurance combination to do both. But in a 1500m race there's so much more patience required, in addition to there being so much more to understand about how a race is developing in front of you.

You can't do much at the start of a 1500m race. As a general rule, if you go out too fast, you'll just die and get swallowed up by your pursuers in the later stages. Sometimes, depending on the draw, you've got to just sit, and then rely on your ability to get yourself into the right place at the right time. Each move has to be carefully plotted out.

Of course there is an extent to which you can learn this kind of patient racecraft by watching videos, practising and experimenting with racing lines until they become second nature. But there's also a degree to which an anxious person like I am, no matter how much they've done in training and how technically skilled they are, just freezes in the throes of a race.

That can happen for any number of reasons. In my case, I've never been someone who likes other people's feet being near mine in a race for example. And in a 1500m race, because there are eight in a race instead of four, that's a lot more people and feet around.

With time to think about it, that kind of peripheral stuff bugs me and gets me edgy in a race. Especially earlier in my career, I've been in situations where I've known exactly what I should do in a race, but just couldn't do it because I froze for some reason.

Equally, in longer races where I've known I'm better than everyone else, I've found my mind wandering. I don't say that to come over as arrogant but sometimes it's clear to everyone that you're the best skater in a heat.

In these situations, while we're skating round, I might find myself losing focus and doing odd things like watching someone else in the race's technique and thinking, *what are they doing? Why exactly are they doing that?* Then I might look at Nick and think, *he looks bored!*

Over shorter distances like the 500m, there just isn't time to let anxiety undermine you and to make you freeze. There's no time to think about anything – you just go. In the 1000m, as long as you're strong enough, you can stay out of trouble more than you ever can in the 1500m.

However, as much as I had experience skating in 1000m and 1500m races and winning medals, and as often as Nick and I disagreed about what my best distance was, it was an undeniable fact that I'd never really been given an opportunity to show what I could do in the 500m.

In fact, my first ever 'A' level 500m final was that Olympic Games in Sochi. And my first 500m race of any kind had been in Olympic qualifying a few months prior, and in that instance it was very tiring because I had to skate in all the events to ensure that I would qualify for the Olympic spot at all. Nevertheless, I went into the games feeling cautiously optimistic about my chances in this brand new discipline.

Where the Olympic 500m competitions are much tougher than other competitions in the sense that, to even be at the Olympics, you've got to be in the top 24 in the world in the first place.

What that means is that, if you get a bad draw in a heat or semi, you could be in serious trouble. Unlike other competitions where you might just be too good for everyone in your race *despite* your draw, at the Olympics there are simply no bad skaters. Inevitably, when combined with the possibility of crashes or DQs, random aspects of the draw means that some top skaters inevitably miss out on the final.

I got to the final of the 500m at Sochi and I remember thinking, *wait I've never been in a 500m final before!*

And I hadn't been – not a World Cup, not a European Championships and not a World Championship. Part of me was a bit confused that I'd made it to one at all, and in it I was going to be skating against one of my rivals, Arianna Fontana from Italy.

By 2014, Arianna and I already had a bit of history. Growing up, she had started skating a lot younger than I did. Everybody raved about her; everybody thought she was amazing.

In truth, historically she was always that bit faster and a better racer than me. But by 2014, we'd switched roles a little. I had started beating her more often than she beat me, most notably in Malmo at the 2013 European Championships where I beat her to win both the 1000m and the 1500m gold medals on my way to the overall silver because she had won the 500m when I fell at the first corner.

Because it was my first, I remember the 500m final at Sochi really well. I remember getting on and thinking, *OK, here we go, Lane 3 – this is a good race for me.*

The reason I was feeling that way was because I knew that the Chinese girl in Lane 4, Li Jianrou, wasn't really a 500m skater. I knew I was way faster than her.

Then in Lane 1 you had the Korean girl who was the

top ranked skater. In all honesty she was really good and I fully expected her to win. And then there was Arianna and I in Lanes 2 and 3 respectively, and at that point, as I said, I didn't think there was much between us.

My game plan was to sit in third and wait until later in the four-lap race to make my move so that I would never be in a position where I could be attacked from behind.

But when we went off the start, I had to change everything because, to my surprise, I was faster in that first lap than Arianna.

In an instant I thought, *OK, I'll just take a position now*, because that gave me the chance to essentially take one of my opponents out of the equation early, and even if she was to pass me later, I reasoned that at least I'd be in third and not fourth.

But, as I went past Arianna on the first straight, she did something that I absolutely didn't expect: she came at me, leaned in on me with her left shoulder with the result being that both she and I went down. Thereafter, the Korean girl, the favourite, also got taken out at the corner.

Meanwhile, the Chinese girl, the least likely winner in my eyes, was left out in front on her own to win the gold medal, while the rest of us picked ourselves up and finished the race miles behind, with me finishing in the silver medal place.

Normally in a situation like that, they'd call the race back, DQ someone, and then run the race again so that it wouldn't be an uncontested race where the only person left in it wins an Olympic gold. That's in the rules, and by that measurement I could still have been kicked out of the race. But they still should have rerun it.

But they didn't do that – and that was one of the many decisions that the referee seemed to get wrong at those games, as far as I saw. He made a load of weird calls, not least in the 1000m final later in the week, where a Chinese girl pulled a Korean girl back as they crossed the line. She used her hands, which you can't do. She should have been disqualified, but for whatever reason she wasn't.

Looking back on the 500m race, and I didn't know this at the time, but the reason Arianna attacked me the way she did was because she only wanted the win. She already had Olympic silver and bronze medals; now she only wanted gold. So her thinking was to stay in second place so that she could attack the leader.

I, on the other hand, with no Olympic medals of any colour to my name, was thinking more defensively in my outlook. Given it was my first 500m final of any kind, I was there primarily to medal. Anything better would have been a huge bonus. So when the incident occurred, all I was thinking was, *if I move into second place now, I'm that much less likely to come fourth!*

On reflection, and I've obviously thought about it a million times since, my view is that race should have been a joint call in the sense that we were both to blame, or not a call at all. As much as my move was a late pass, I didn't change direction as I passed Arianna. But she changed direction when she leaned into me, and technically speaking that was an illegal move.

Truthfully, it's the kind of move that any of us might consider making at a World Cup where there are always plenty of races. With multiple races coming thick and fast over several days, World Cup meetings are a lot more laid back in that sense. If you fell, you'd pretty much pick yourself up, laugh and say, "There's always tomorrow!"

But at an Olympic Games, there is no tomorrow. There's just one final and short track immortality awaits the winner of it. It's a completely different situation. I thought that what Arianna did was a risk not worth taking.

Anyway, I remember skating over to Nick after the race. At that point, as much as I knew there'd been this massive crash, I was still 50/50 in my head about what the eventual ruling was going to be.

Part of me believed I'd just won an Olympic silver medal, albeit in admittedly unsatisfactory circumstances. Even the British commentator apparently said something along the lines of, "Great Britain's Elise Christie has just won an Olympic silver medal!"

Even he didn't appear to think the crash was my fault.

I really thought that they wouldn't call it in my favour and so I looked at Nick for a bit of a steer.

"I don't know, Elise," he said, as if he was questioning my role in the whole thing.

I'd never heard him say anything like that before. I'd never heard Nick Gooch sound unsure about anything in eight years of knowing him. He'd normally just give me a straight answer – good or bad.

When he didn't, I just burst into tears. I didn't know what else to do.

It was the weirdest experience to be standing there about to either win an Olympic silver medal or to have one taken away because of a disqualification. And the decision took what seemed like forever because it was a complex call. As I was standing there trying to be calm, behind the scenes my mind was going hyper. I just kept thinking to myself, *please. Please!*

And then they called the penalty on me. In an instant, the medal was gone.

On one hand I was devastated to have just come second and lost it. That hurt like hell. But another part of me, as much as the situation absolutely sucked, acknowledged that it was my first ever 500m final, I hadn't expected to be there in the first place, and that it was only my first event of the Olympics.

Nevertheless, I came off the ice and went into the media still pretty upset about everything. Then I got pulled straight into doping as one of the random post-race checks, which felt like a right kick in the arse given what had just happened.

I was in there for a couple of hours and then I went into the athlete lounge where Jack and a few others including Nick were sitting just chilling out, playing on the PlayStation – and doing some terrible singing in those little karaoke booths as I recall – because everyone had the next day off. As much as I wanted to stew over it, I just couldn't; it wouldn't have been constructive. The way I rationalised it away in that moment, in order to move on mentally, was by telling myself that Nick was actually right and that the 500m wasn't my best distance after all.

At the same time I told myself that I was still on form and still the strongest person there. In my head I had two more good chances.

I thought, *I'll move on. Let's get on with it.*

"Where's my phone?' I said.

Somebody handed it me.

At that point Nick turned around.

"I suggest that you don't go on your phone," Nick said.

"What? Why?" I replied.

I went on my phone and when I did I had this feeling like the one you get when you go over a hill in your car. As I started to scroll, my stomach just dropped to the floor.

"Oh my fucking god," I whispered.

As I said, I was over it.

But what I realised was that the online world felt differently.

On one hand I could see that I was getting dogs abuse from the British public on Twitter for being crap, and that they shouldn't be funding me because I was so shit. Up until that point I hardly used Twitter and only ever went on there because Team GB told us to beforehand.

And then I scrolled through Facebook…

Prior to the games, I'd only ever used Facebook for

chatting to friends and having a laugh. However, in the immediate build-up to the Olympics, a new 'official' page was created for me and when I looked through that, all I saw were about another 10,000 comments from Koreans.

To my horror, they were taking a different angle to the British people. And it wasn't pretty.

Some were saying that they wanted to kill me, that if I went to Korea they'd bloody kill me, and that they wanted to kill my mum.

I stood there with my phone in my hand staring at the screen in disbelief thinking, *what? Why?*

Immediately I thought of those stories you read in the papers about celebrities who get their house trashed or get physically attacked by people who just don't like them.

In that moment I thought, *this is going to be me. I'm going to get... killed.*

I genuinely thought that my life as I had known it was over.

I don't mind saying that the abuse from the British public didn't even make any sense to me at all. What they didn't know was that there were plenty of other people there at the Olympics, funded as I was, and that they'd never even heard of. Some of them were finishing bloody 19th and 24th in their events. And yet they were heroes?

Meanwhile, there I was getting annihilated for messing up in an elite final that involved the top four skaters in the world. It didn't seem fair and I wanted to get stuck right in and start talking sense into a few people online.

My typing fingers were poised and my jaw was set. I was ready to let some people have a piece of my mind.

But then Nick stepped in.

"Just ignore them. If you respond it'll only make it worse," he told me.

Of course, what he said was logical, and I knew that Nick was only upset because he could see how much all of this was hurting me – to be being abused about the one thing, skating, on which my entire self-value relied.

But he was also experienced enough to know that by engaging with so much negativity, I'd only be inviting more abuse. If he'd been in my situation, given his confidence and ignorance/ intolerance of social media, it wouldn't have bothered Nick at all.

"I get it, but ignore it. They're just sitting there online. We need to move forward," he said.

Initially, because I was less experienced and am more sensitive, I thought, *but are they just sitting there online though?*

As hard as it is for the public to physically get to an athlete at an Olympic Games, I knew there were Koreans in Sochi and I was terrified because I really had no idea how organised or credible those online death threats were.

As it turned out (although I only found this out after the games) protection in the form of covert security had already swooped in. For the rest of the games, I'm told that one of MI5 or MI6, I'm not sure which, followed me around watching my every move and watched exactly what was being said when I was trending on Twitter. I guess they had to take the threats seriously.

In any case, having talked to a few officials at the BOA, one of them a clinical psychologist, I reached a point the next day where I started feeling secure in the village with my friends and teammates around me. I started believing that nothing was going to happen while I was there anyway and that the whole thing would probably blow over soon enough.

This feeling was reinforced by the fact that, by the time we'd got to a couple of days later, just before the 1500m final, I'd received many messages from other Korean girls that I'd skated with who all wanted to show me their support and to say, regarding the online trolls, "We can't believe how they're behaving. Just ignore them".

At the same time, even the Korean girl who'd been knocked over in the 500m final came up to me and gave me a big hug because she felt so bad about what her country's people were doing to me. Her sympathy was totally genuine; she was a good friend to me.

But there was a twist in the tail of that sympathetic gesture.

Because she had been the favourite in the 500m and hadn't won it, she now didn't want to skate in the 1500m because she wanted to focus all her attention on the last event, the 1000m, instead. "I think I'm going to just pull out of the 1500m," she told me.

What she told me and what she later told the media

were two different things. I knew she wasn't a long distance skater and that it made total sense for her to focus her attention on her best chance of a gold medal in the 1000m. In her shoes, I might have done the same.

But what she told the media was that she'd hurt herself in the collision in the 500m – a collision that the whole world knew I'd been disqualified for causing.

It just wasn't true.

She hadn't hurt herself. But her comment to the press really dropped me deeper in the shit.

That's where the real backlash started coming back at me.

"Because of you, our skater can't compete in the 1500m Olympic final," one message said.

"You injured our athlete," was another.

"Only you are to blame…" yet another

There were countless more. I stopped reading them.

As all of these accusations were still raging in the background, all I could think at that point was, *fucking hell! I know why your athlete isn't in the 1500m final because she has already told me she doesn't want to be!*

It was all such a mess, and as if that wasn't bad enough, I recall hearing that I was also getting some abuse from Italians online too – albeit much less of it. The situation wasn't helped by something Arianna said in the media afterwards, when she referred to what I'd done as something along the lines of a "stupid move".

As much as she too had been nice to my face in light of

the vicious backlash I was getting, I was still disappointed by that comment of hers

As a speed skater, and one who had made plenty of stupid moves at various times herself, I thought what she said was a bit cheeky given how close a call it had been. It was far from a clear-cut decision. *She* could have easily been thrown out for moving into me so aggressively. *She* didn't need to do what she did. We could have *all* stayed in that race.

Anyway, amidst this total sideshow rumbling on about the 500m final, I somehow managed to build myself back up for the 1500m. As much as I still didn't see it as my best tactical distance – despite what Nick thought – I'd done a lot of 1500m races in competition so I still went into it feeling as confident of doing well as I had prior to the 500m.

As it turned out, I got quite a tough draw in the first round even though I knew I was stronger than them all. One of them was Arianna, and with two laps to go we'd pulled well clear of the others.

Before the race, I clearly remember Nick saying, "If you can win, win". His reasoning behind that was that by winning I'd maybe have a chance of getting a better draw in the next round.

But then he also said, "But if there's any risk of causing a crash, don't do it".

So there I was, sitting in there behind Arianna with two laps to go finding it ridiculously easy. I was cruising.

In general, skating behind rather than leading feels so much easier. Out in front, as you're forging ahead and controlling the race pace, you can feel the air and actually hear it going past your head. You're aware of environmental vagaries like humidity and air pressure out there to the extent that you can even tell whether you're in a fast environment or a slow one just by how the air *sounds*.

But behind, you experience none of this. Instead, you just follow along in the leader's slipstream. It's eerily quiet. But to win, you know you've got to pass at some point.

As easy as I was finding it in Arianna's slipstream for all the above reasons, I was still reluctant to pass her because of Nick's warning. As comfortable as I was, the events of the previous day were still fresh in my mind. Rather than moving too soon, I decided to wait and go at her just as we approached the winning line. I knew that my ability to accelerate suddenly would be enough to get me there.

As the line loomed ahead, I went.

It was all calculated to the inch. I even made sure to leave loads of space so that I didn't touch her as I passed and, equally, to make sure there was no way she could come across me. Given what had happened in the 500m, I wanted there to be zero possibility for controversy. It all worked perfectly. I finished the race, won the race, got my skates off and walked into the media. I was bloody buzzing.

"Why have you been penalised?' someone said.

"What do you mean?" I replied.

I had no idea I'd even been penalised. In my mind I

knew that it had been the cleanest possible race. I had never touched anyone. I thought there must have been a mistake.

All the media kept asking me the same question, and I started to feel stupid because I gave everyone in the media zone the exact same answer – that I didn't have any answers and that I had no idea about being penalised!

Just as I walked out of the media zone, Nick came over to me.

"You didn't actually cross the finish line," he said.

"What are you talking about?" I replied. "What do you mean I didn't cross the finish line?"

"The chief referee is saying you were a millimetre inside the line," Nick explained.

"But that never gets called!" I protested.

Electronically I'd crossed the finish line because my time came up on the screen. But apparently when they looked at the photo finish – a photo finish that only bloody existed at all because I had decided to grab the win close to the line – they claimed that I hadn't actually breached it.

What didn't make sense was that this kind of minute technicality doesn't normally get called in short track. Not. Ever. Normally, as long as a skater's time comes up on the screen, everything is fine. In fact, at the European Championships a month later, someone didn't cross the finish line in the semi-final and still went on to win the gold medal.

I, on the other hand, would win no medal. My time came

up, but I was being disqualified from the 1500m instead. All because of a millimetre – even though my performance director Stuart Horsepool was frantically running around trying to get them to re-measure the actual line on the ice to prove that the measurement was even accurate.

Meanwhile, I heard that Wilf O'Reilly, who was working as an analyst for the BBC, had said something to the effect that he had never seen a decision like it in all his years of short track speed skating. And this was a guy who'd won two gold medals for Britain at the 1988 Olympics in Calgary as part of a great skating career.

The officials weren't having any of it though. As far as they were concerned, while I'd triggered the precise electronic sensor, I apparently hadn't crossed an inexact physical line painted on the ice. As ridiculous as it might sound, that was their position and they weren't moving from it.

In the end, despite all the protests, I was out of the 1500m in the heats.

As much as I was annoyed to have been disqualified from my second consecutive event at an Olympic Games, there was a more far-reaching issue that I couldn't ignore.

I thought the whole line controversy matter made the sport of short track look really stupid and must have made our sport's rules appear ambiguous – at best – to anyone watching on TV at home. In a minority sport that already had a big enough task on its hands attracting interest, that was the last thing short track needed. It was a terrible call in my opinion, both from a personal perspective and a PR one.

After getting disqualified from the 1500m, I mentioned something to the media about having received death threats online. It was a throwaway line said from a place of great pain and disappointment. But the media certainly took notice.

By this point, my agent at Octagon was handling all of my social media accounts anyway; I had nothing to do with them and from that point of view I'm sure there was a lot of horrible stuff that I never saw.

I should say that I didn't particularly want to stay off social media. I just didn't think that it was the right thing to do. But I trusted their decision nevertheless, and went along with it.

But what I soon found out from my agent was that, after me telling the media about the death threats, there had been a big swing in public opinion from the people in the UK. I hadn't known any of this and I guess I had assumed that I was still just getting abuse.

Suddenly, having been the villain, the funded waste of space with no ability, apparently I was now being lauded by what seemed like 90 per cent of UK fans. Instead of all the hate, I started getting nice messages and posts expressing support, from both friends and strangers alike.

Up until that point, very few of my close friends even knew that I'd been being bullied online. Obviously they'd have seen the races and clearly they must have known that I was on the tough end of a couple of bad decisions.

But for many of them, I'm sure they just saw it all and thought, *that's just sport*. But when I went public about the fact I'd been bullied and threatened – everything changed. Loads of people started contacting me because, suddenly, it had become about so much more than sport.

Honestly, after the 1500m, I'd been pretty close to just giving up altogether. I couldn't see how the Sochi Olympics could possibly have gotten any worse for me. But those messages really changed the momentum and gave me a real boost, even though the long-term psychological damage was probably already done. From wanting to bail from the 1000m altogether and call it a day, I decided at the time that I'd get myself mentally up for it and go again.

I thought, *well, I've got a reason to do this now.*

It was no longer just about me, but about the whole country. It was the first time in my career that I'd ever felt the incredible power of patriotism flowing through me.

And so, with the words, "Look, Elise, it can't happen three times in a row," still ringing in my ears from the final conversation with my psychologist before I got on the ice, it was onwards to the 1000m.

Being my best distance, I went through the heats of the 1000m and blasted everybody.

In the quarter-finals I qualified easily, having gone around the outside of the girl who ultimately won the competition. I dropped her like she wasn't even there.

Come on!!! I thought, as I crossed the line.

In the semis I had a really tough draw, with two Chinese girls and a Korean, but at that point I was on a roll of unshakeable confidence thinking, *do you know what? I'm just going to do the same thing again: I'm going around the outside, staying out of trouble, then I'll move at the finish.*

It all started well. I flew round the outside of the Chinese girl and dropped her. That was her essentially out of the race. Then I went up the inside of the other Chinese girl. I cleanly went past her, but as I did, she dived into the corner and fell over in my slipstream, bringing me down from behind in the process by knocking my feet away. For good measure, she also half-grabbed me with her arms from behind whereupon I slid out the side too. When it happened, I immediately thought, *that's OK, not a big deal. I'll get advanced.*

It was one of those situations where, although she wasn't certain to get a penalty, I was equally certain to be advanced because she had brought me down.

I got off the ice, started taking my skates off and as I was sitting in the heat-box (an enclosed area for competitors before and after races) I remember turning around to my physio who was sitting behind me.

"Wouldn't it be funny if he gave me another penalty?!" I said, half laughing. "Stop being silly!" he said.

Everyone knew I'd get advanced. And at that point the only thing that was worrying me was that when I did get advanced there'd be five people in the final instead of four, and I'd be stuck out there in Lane 5 because of my slow time.

And then it came up on the screen that we'd *both* got a penalty.

Is this a wind up? I thought.

Funny, right? Wrong…

I couldn't believe what I was seeing. It didn't make any sense. They gave us both the same penalty because of one overtaking manoeuvre. You can't do that! It goes against all the rules of short track. But that's what that American referee did.

At this point I was basically feeling, again, that my life was all over. Here I was in a sport that had attracted me specifically because the outcome should, in theory, never be subjective. Yet, in the space of a few days, I'd been on the end of three calls that were entirely subjective – all at one Olympics. You couldn't make it up! I'd bloody had enough.

Nick tried his best to pick me up. "There's always another Olympics. There's more to life than short track, you know," he said.

But I didn't want to hear any of that phony inspirational stuff. So instead of listening to any more of it, I went back to the village and decided to go out and get blind drunk with Eve Muirhead and her girls' curling team, who were in the process of celebrating their bronze medal.

As much as I knew that getting smashed wasn't exactly the most constructive of responses, I just wanted to blank everything out for a while. I wanted to escape the Olympics; the shocking decisions and the ire of the internet trolls. And for the few hours of that Sochi evening it felt good to do so. The next morning, given how much of a lightweight I am when it comes to drink, I really didn't feel so good.

SIX

SLIPPING

ALTHOUGH THE TIDE OF PUBLIC OPINION had predominantly turned to positivity, when I left Sochi, my agent and support team turned all my social media off completely anyway. I absolutely didn't agree with that decision.

I thought it showed weakness on my part. The way I saw it, when people – in this case random members of the British public – went online and started abusing someone, they wanted to see weakness. That's why they were doing it. I just felt that if I went dark because of it, I'd just be showing the haters all the weakness they wanted. With no means of responding, in effect I'd be saying, *OK, you've won.*

Although the intensity progressively died down day-by-day, even once I'd been back in the UK for a few days, the abuse hadn't completely stopped. I remember doing an interview shortly after I returned to England and I later heard that there were the same negative and abusive reactions to that one posted online. Stuff about me being useless and a waste of funding – all those kinds of things.

What I realised at that moment was that life probably wasn't ever going to be the same. Before Sochi, I was a relative unknown outside of my minority sport. All I had was a few hundred followers on Instagram who enjoyed seeing my posts and pictures. I didn't have to deal with much in the way of public scrutiny because the majority of the wider public simply didn't know who I was.

But the very public way in which the Sochi games played out changed all of that. And I realised that from that week onwards that I was probably going to have to navigate my life differently going forward. Not only that, I knew that I was going to need other people to help manage me too, just to keep me sane.

As it turned out, with a week and a half until the World Championships in Montreal, it worked out OK in that I didn't have to worry about what was happening on social media. I could keep focusing on skating and in that moment it meant I could dedicate all of my mental energy on getting ready for the Worlds instead of worrying about the bigger picture of my public image. To that end, I literally started training again the day I landed in England from Sochi.

And it worked, because I went to Montreal more determined than ever and got a silver medal in the 500m on the way to fourth place overall.

The only annoying aspect of those World Championships

was that, after having gone and won a medal straight after the disappointment of Sochi, I couldn't share it with people I wanted to post about it online as if to say, "Look what I can do under a different referee!"

On one hand I wanted to show my supportive fans that Sochi had been merely bad luck. On another I suppose a bigger part of me wanted to stick one right up all of the haters. But I couldn't do either.

It was only when I returned from the Montreal Worlds that I really started feeling the full weight of what had happened in Sochi.

Like any traumatic experience, I think you go through phases afterwards: shock, denial, acceptance and the like. But in my case, all of those kinds of emotions had always been obscured in previous instances by the fact that I had skating to focus on to distract me.

But now, without skating, alone in my house with just my thoughts and insecurities for company, things became much more difficult in 2014 and even into 2015. The ironic thing is that, immediately prior to Sochi, I remember hearing about the Olympic gymnast Beth Tweddle getting a load of online abuse after appearing on a Sky Sports Q and A.

At that time, I'm not sure I took it that seriously. I'm sure even I just thought, *why doesn't she just ignore it?*

But when it's you, you can't ignore it – that's the difference that you don't understand as an outsider. You don't really notice these things at the time, but I know that I started withdrawing from what had been normal life. I spoke to people less and I went outside as infrequently as possible. I was always just too scared to put myself into any social setting for fear of someone trying to get to me.

As irrational as it might sound, I still found myself thinking, *what if one of those online haters was serious?*

Given there were so many people online saying they wanted to harm me, I just couldn't dismiss the fear that just one of them might try to do something.

On reflection, and again I didn't specifically identify each component at the time, I think a number of events in my life were manifesting at once to put me in this new and elevated state of fear and anxiety.

Obviously, I'd always been an anxious person to a degree, all the way back to primary school in Scotland. But when you added in a rape, a near-fatal house fire and now all the trauma of online abuse at Sochi, the combined effect was just too much for me to handle at that time.

Although I knew that the events of Sochi had definitely been the trigger, I also realised that the unresolved emotions attached to these other real-life events were all just as significant in terms of their role in putting me in this unwelcome place.

Not just that, because these events had actually *happened* to me in real life. I was physically bullied, the rape in 2010 happened and the apartment really did catch fire in 2012. I could go on and on.

These things were all tangible events that did me material harm, and I think there was part of me that feared that someone acting on an online threat wasn't such a far-fetched possibility either.

For a while, fear stopped me functioning. On the few occasions I did summon the courage to put myself into any kind of social group, I remember feeling completely unable to communicate. I couldn't start a conversation and I couldn't focus on anyone else's. The whole time I was there, all I'd be thinking about was when I could leave. My friends had no idea how to relate to me.

On one hand, anxiety is just so debilitating. I had regular panic attacks, lost social connections and just couldn't calm my mind for more than five seconds at a time.

But the upside, if you can call it that, was that I definitely got a lot of housework done in my apartment, which wasn't something I was exactly renowned for up until that point.

Suddenly, I found myself constantly cleaning, washing, dusting and what have you – sometimes into the early hours of the morning. I wasn't quite dusting apples, bananas or my cats, but it was close.

Looking back now, it was certainly a bit manic at times, but it was all I could do to distract myself from these constant feelings of fear and anxiety that the online abuse had triggered.

By the summer of 2014 then, I existed in a world of perpetual anxiety in my personal life.

As much as I was with Jack, I didn't want to discuss my feelings with him and I certainly didn't want to talk about any of it with my mother or, in fact, anyone else.

Instead, I did the only thing I knew that could save me. To counteract everything that was wrong about my private life, I started putting even more than I ever had into my skating existence.

As an interesting precursor to the PyeongChang Olympics that were still three and a half years away, I was actually sent out to South Korea by Team GB in 2014, a few months after the Sochi games.

On paper it was a legitimate training camp that lasted three months, but on another level the team wanted to show me that, no matter what had happened online at Sochi, I would be fine when I eventually competed in South Korea and that any threats to kill me were merely the work of anonymous keyboard warriors with nothing better to do, as opposed to being the work of real people with strong grievances that they were prepared to act upon in 'real life'.

As it turned out, it was a valuable trip and a bit of a long-range pre-2018 Olympics PR exercise that worked both ways. At the time I was so anxious about being there. I was a wreck to start with. But it soon became apparent that the realities of the situation were so different from the picture I'd created in my mind.

Wherever I went I got stopped and asked for autographs and pictures. Everything was positive and the people were so friendly and welcoming. The trip really opened my eyes to the reality that, as much as people might write things online in the heat of the moment, a lot of the time they don't mean it and never think about the consequences of what they type beyond whatever fleeting satisfaction they got the moment they pressed 'send'. People even said, "I'm sorry about the way my country behaved".

Don't get me wrong, I'm sure there are still Korean skating fans out there that don't like me and I do still get the occasional abusive message to this day. But the trip to PyeongChang really made me understand that everything isn't always as it seems. As much as there might have been a ton of notifications on my phone when I came off the ice that night in Sochi, the reality is that, as intimidating as it felt, it was still just a tiny minority relative to the number of normal people out there who'd never dream of abusing someone they don't know online.

By the autumn, with the European Championships in Holland looming in January 2015 and the World Championships in Moscow scheduled for two months later, I was absolutely flying again on the ice.

Despite everything, my skating was arguably as good as it had ever been and I can only put this down to my ability not to separate these two distinct parts of my life (that would have been impossible), but instead to leverage one off the other and use my ability to be good at skating to hold the anxiety and low self-worth at bay.

This tactic worked. Despite my anxiety leading to a fundamental and primal fear of relay races because of all the noise that comes with them at the start, I was great in the Europeans, winning a gold in the 500m and the 1500m,

ELISE CHRISTIE

and similarly good at the Worlds where I won two silvers in the 500m and the 1000m respectively

But then, as good a start to 2015 as I'd had on ice, my boyfriend Jack and I split up not long after I got back from the World Championships in Moscow. It was my doing; I thought the relationship hadn't been working.

With hindsight, we'd reached a point after almost five years together where I wondered where it was all going. At various points along the way I thought he might propose to me but he never did.

To be honest, I think I saw that as a bit of a red flag at the time, even though when I asked myself questions like, "If he did propose, what would I say?" I wasn't even sure what my answer would be. I asked myself, *at this point shouldn't I be sure?*

Also, and this was bad on my behalf, Jack genuinely went off the rails a bit after Sochi because of his issues with his skating. But at that time I was too young to understand what was going on and I thought, *well, none of this is good for my career.*

Looking back, that was a bit insensitive of me and I regret that. Jack clearly wasn't doing well, but because I just didn't know any better, instead of helping, I just thought, *what the hell is wrong with him?*

As break-ups go it was a bloody messy one, but not for the usual reasons like abuse or because someone was cheating. In those situations it's much easier to break up with someone, I guess. Jack didn't do anything bad, but I still couldn't really give him a specific reason for why I was ending it other than I had this feeling – maybe it was a woman's intuition – that the relationship had run its course.

Where it became even more difficult was that having split up after living together for years – sharing everything including a mortgage together – we were still on the same skating programme. No matter how awful and raw we felt, we still had to walk in there and see each other every day. It wasn't easy at the time and it took a while – probably a full year – until the emotions dissipated enough that we could start being friends again.

Nowadays we're totally fine. We see each other all the time. He's got a really nice girlfriend and I think they'll probably end up getting married one day.

I'm sure it didn't help matters for Jack that it wasn't long after he and I split that I bounced straight into another relationship, after a meeting at the Invitation Cup in Dresden in October 2015.

Although I didn't know him and had never spoken to him, Hungarian skater Shaolin Sándor Liu had been around during my career ever since he first came on the short track scene in 2012. To be honest, in my view he always had the rep of being a bit of a player – a ladies man or whatever else.

However, out of the blue and not long after Jack and I broke up, Shaolin approached me online and started giving me some chat. Initially, I was averse to the idea of a relationship at all. I was still in the aftermath of a messy break-up with Jack and was wary of rebounding to someone else when the person who was most in need of my care and love was myself.

Beyond that, I just thought Shaolin was just too young. I was 25 at the time and he hadn't quite turned 20. I was also well aware of his reputation and couldn't help but think, *I'm just not interested.*

However, Shaolin was unusually kind and persistent – in addition to being an undeniably good-looking lad. To be fair to him, over quite a good couple of months he put in some serious and respectful grind. For ages he was chasing me online and eventually we started talking on Facetime.

It developed from there to the point where I started changing my tune and thinking, *you know what? He deserves a chance after the effort he's put in...*

The first time we were with each other properly was at that Invitation Cup in Dresden in September 2015. We didn't do anything physically or anything; we just talked. But at the World Cup meeting in Toronto a few weeks later, that's when he asked me to officially be his girlfriend.

Looking back now, because our relationship started long distance – me in Nottingham and him in Hungary – and given how developed messaging and video calling was by then, being at a distance was never really a problem because that's all we ever knew.

Also, given that we were both professional athletes who travelled around the world to the same meetings annually – World Cups, Europeans, World Championships and, every four years, an Olympics – it all worked OK in the sense that we had each other as well as having our own parallel elite careers to focus on.

What is certain is that I was of great help to Shaolin in terms of advice and experience for his career. As backward as I thought the UK programme was at times, Hungary was in the absolute dark ages when it came to aspects of sports science like psychology, nutrition and general strength and conditioning methods.

Because I was that much older and already had almost 10 years experience at the top level, there's no doubt that, as much as there was definitely a deep romantic connection between us, there were other benefits for him on a career level associated with dating me. All of this I knew and was fine with at the time because we were still in that place where our romantic feelings for each other eclipsed everything else. Love is blind and all that…

In March 2016, I went to the World Championships in Seoul skating well on paper but was in a terrible mental place again.

I wouldn't say I was depressed per se, but I was certainly anxious all the time. Even though I was in a new relationship, my self-esteem felt like it was at an all-time low and I realised that I was putting too much pressure on my skating to prop everything up.

As an inherently anxious person, I was always at my best when I skated fearlessly with absolutely no inhibitions. It was in those moments when I felt the most joy, and it was when I felt joy that I won the most races and, by extension, felt the best about myself afterwards. Skating without fear fed a self-perpetuating cycle of positivity.

But by 2016, a shift was under way.

As dominant as I had been at Sochi in the Europeans in January, where I won gold in all three distances and won overall gold, and as much as it definitely felt good to be able to partially bury the ghost of 2014, albeit at a lesser Championships, I had reached a point at those World Championships in Seoul where I could envisage the fear of losing held me back. And the reason I could was that I knew what failure would do to my shaky self-esteem: I'd hate myself.

That's how it played out. It was a self-fulfilling prophecy. I went out in the quarter-finals of the 500m in an event ultimately won by the Chinese girl, Fan Kexin.

In the 1000m final, another final I should have won, I came second to Choi the Korean girl, ironically, because I feared losing too much. Then I was third in the 1500m.

On one hand I was absolutely raging with myself. I was skating well but I was also skating scared. On the other, I was struggling with this constantly high level of anxiety that made me think, *I just can't go on like this. I can't let fear stop me achieving my potential.*

Eventually the time came to seek proper professional help and in 2016, UK Sport sent me to The Priory to talk it over with someone.

I didn't think I was depressed, but at that time I didn't even know what depression was. I think I just went with what a lot of people thought at that time: that depression was simply somebody's choice to be sad.

Obviously, I know much more nowadays; everyone's awareness of mental health is so much greater than it was five years ago. But at the time, I just wanted any help, even though I wasn't exactly certain what I needed help with.

After seeing that clinical psychologist at The Priory in late 2016, I left with a diagnosis of PTSD and promptly did what a lot of people do when they get diagnosed with a mental health condition: I went into denial.

To be fair, I didn't know much about what PTSD was anyway. I just thought it was something only soldiers came back with after fighting wars.

Consequently – and despite having talked openly to the specialist at length as he listened to the evidence (some of which wasn't unlike fighting in a bloody war when you analysed it) – I left the consultation feeling strangely better, even if my first thoughts after being diagnosed were, *yeah sure, I get it… but that's not me.*

Looking back, that was a ridiculously naïve, not to mention conflicted, response of mine. I mean, on paper, who'd had more intense and varied types of trauma than I'd had in 26 years of living? If anyone was entitled to be suffering from post-traumatic stress, surely it was me?

But for whatever reason, I didn't want to acknowledge the PTSD diagnosis at that time – and I certainly didn't want to hear that the specialist also suspected that I might also be heading towards being depressive. Depression, in my eyes, was completely out of the question. I didn't want that label, and I never went back. The Priory was a disaster as far as I was concerned.

Having said all this, although I didn't take any real ownership of the clinical psychologist's advice at the time, on reflection I do think that the act of talking to someone about my problems for the first time was of real benefit to me at that moment in my life.

The fact that it wasn't somebody I knew or who knew me – a boyfriend, coach, a best friend or a family member – and was a total stranger instead, meant that I definitely derived quite a bit of encouragement from the fact that I could at least open up and talk at all. That was at least a first.

While I wasn't quite at the stage where I was prepared to tackle anything head-on, in late 2016, with a permanent resolution in mind, I did get the kind of boost I needed to launch myself into the World Championships in Rotterdam in March 2017.

Prior to Rotterdam, a freak accident in training turned into something of a blessing in disguise. Six weeks before the competition, I collided head-on with a post in a warm-up session shortly after the New Year. It was my fault and a stupid mistake, and the concussion meant that I was out for six weeks and would miss the European Championships in Turin in the middle of January. Initially I thought, *well shit, that's my World Championship hopes down the drain.*

But a week before the Worlds, I was back and ready to compete. On one level I was semi-panicking because I hadn't done much for a month and felt that I'd be arriving undercooked.

On another, I suppose the concussion took the pressure off me in the sense that I went to those World Championships not expecting a whole lot. Given the head injury and the stipulated recovery time afterwards, I was just happy to be able to skate at all in Rotterdam.

From a mindset perspective, when I started thinking about actual racing, I realised that there were aspects of the conversation with the clinical psychologist that had clearly stuck. And the most tangible impact these conversations had on me was that I now understood that the simple act of off-loading had allowed me to switch my mindset away from the hopeless state of being so scared to lose that I couldn't skate at all.

I wouldn't say that I went into those 2017 World Championships not caring about outcomes, but I certainly went in there feeling that winning a medal wasn't a life-or-death situation.

In my head I said to myself, *you've already got a load of medals at different championships. What difference is another going to make?*

I wasn't thinking any of this from a position of arrogance – not at all.

I didn't take any of my previous medals for granted and I'd had to exceed all expectations to get them given I was coming from a team culture that wasn't accustomed to winning medals regularly. All I was doing was taking the pressure off. I was giving myself permission to skate with no fear of failure.

Weirdly, I went into the competition as the so-called "fastest woman on ice", having broken the world record for 500m in the World Cup meeting in Salt Lake City a few months earlier. To celebrate it, they put up a banner at the National Ice Centre in Nottingham. That said, I went to Rotterdam with the 1000m as my primary target, not the 500m.

In the 500m final I got drawn in Lane 1, which was a decent outcome given that I knew that if I got off the start quickly, there was a good chance I'd be able to lead and stay there.

As it turned out, both me and the Chinese girl in Lane 4 got called for false starts and from there I was on the back foot. On the restart I didn't get off the start particularly well and was just never in the race.

In the 1500m final, I was drawn out wide in Lane 6 and pretty much decided right away that I was going to get off the start and sit wherever I ended up after the first bend, which turned out to be in last place.

If you get a final with a lot of top people in it, quite often you'll find that they'll go really slow because everyone's trying to conserve energy. That happens less if you get a final where a few have been disqualified along the way, leaving only two or three of the top girls in the final.

However that 1500m final in 2017 was absolutely as good as it possibly could have been. It was one of the best races I've ever skated in and so, true to form, we went very slowly off the start.

However, Nick always had a rule for when it was slow like that and that was: "At seven or eight laps to go, you need to be near the front" – the reasoning being that if you wait too long, people will be skating so fast that you'll just never get past anyone. Even the statistics bore that theory out. They showed that you've really got to always be in the first four to have a chance to medal.

With eight laps left, I made a pretty bold move around the outside and into the lead. From there I dictated the race, skating at the equivalent of 500m race pace on what was a pretty slow rink to start with.

While doing that, I knew that unless someone was ridiculously fast they weren't getting past me easily, given that I was skating both very quick and on defensive lines (pulling tight on the entry to the bends from a wide position to stop someone going outside).

Even while I was out in front and controlling who could attack me, given it was a 1500m race, I wasn't sure I was going to win. But I knew, with six or seven to go, that I'd medal for sure if I didn't fall or get bumped. Then, when I got to one to go, I thought, *I'm winning this!* I couldn't believe what was happening.

Despite a last corner scare when one of the Korean girls who'd earlier been hit and spun out of the race needed a hefty shove out of the way from me as I lapped her, I was almost there. For a second there was a moment of mild panic as I realised that, with the lapped Korean temporarily in my path taking all my space and speed (having been told to do just that by her coach to help her teammate win the race), the Canadian girl was eyeing an opportunity to nick up the inside.

Thankfully I just held on to win my first ever World Championship gold medal. The Canadian, Marianne St-Gelais, thought she'd won, but when I stuck my toe out at the line, I *knew* I'd won. Best of all, I'd won it a year ahead of the eight-year plan.

The Korean girl got a penalty after the race but we all thought she should have been red carded for cheating. That could have been my only ever World Championship gold medal and I could have lost it because someone cheated me out of it. If that had happened I would have flipped a lid. I'd have probably punched someone! Thankfully it never did come to that.

Going into the 1000m a day later I felt like all the pressure was off me. I was so relieved that I'd already won an unexpected gold in the 1500m. Regardless, I was pretty confident that I'd win the 1000m anyway.

We had also done a bit of statistical research on the 1000m and when we crunched all the numbers it transpired that you really needed to be in the first two for the entire race. Then, beyond that, we were shocked to discover that over 90 per cent of the winners of top 1000m races were leading with four laps to go.

As it turned out, the two Koreans tried to skate against

me to stop me getting to the front. So I skated patiently, didn't get involved in any fights, and then right at the end I used all the speed I'd saved.

Compared to most girls, I had this ability to accelerate suddenly. They always said I was more like a man in that respect. And because of this trait, I didn't necessarily have to be leading or even in the first two with four to go. I could get round the outside of people late in races. And with just two of us left in the race for the gold medal, I did just that. I proved that I was the exception to these overwhelming statistics. Everyone else had been blown out of the water.

Even then, having hit the front, the Korean girl Choi still tried to smack me going around the last corner. For a second I actually thought I was going down with the winning line in sight; I was two hands down on the ice for an instant, which is obviously a pretty desperate position to be in. But I managed to salvage it to win my second gold, while Choi got disqualified.

I signed off for the 2017 off-season as a double world champion gold medallist and the overall world champion.

In the short track skating world, a world champion is often held in higher regard than an Olympic gold medallist. From a funding perspective, both are equally as valuable in the eyes of UK Sport. At an Olympics, it's just one race and somebody could get either lucky or unlucky, as I did at Sochi. Short track is an absolutely brutal sport in that regard.

But to be world champion, and the first British or

European to do so, there's no luck involved. A skater has to go out there and prove it and in 2017 I was in the form of my life and I did exactly that. I broke the Asian stranglehold on women's short track skating.

I was so elated on the ice that I couldn't even process what had just happened. At first I screamed at the top of my voice – a rare thing for me, believe me. Then I skated over to Nick and we both burst into tears. Our eight-year plan was paying huge dividends, and I was ahead of schedule.

SEVEN

ALARM BELLS

AFTER THE OFF-SEASON THAT YEAR, starting from the beginning of July 2017, I'd been getting up every morning to train but I was feeling real pain in the outside of my right leg.

For me, this was a completely new sensation. I'd always considered myself to be a very robust athlete. I didn't break down under duress; I'd always had the appetite to be able to take really heavy loads of training.

Furthermore, as I've said before, I'd like to think that I know my own body inside out. Chronic discomfort, therefore, was a major alarm bell for me that wouldn't stop ringing.

With hindsight, the reason for the pain wasn't too hard to figure out. Since coming back into training at the beginning of May after the highs of the World Championships in Rotterdam in March, instead of me working on alternate days between middle and top-level skaters – I'd been training full-time with the top boys.

The difference in the two regimes from a physical perspective is huge and, on the surface, I was still able to produce results in training, day in and day out. My mental toughness helped me keep that intensity going for essentially three months straight.

People who don't know the sport understandably assume that short track training involves putting skates on, getting on the ice and then just skating round in circles for hours. Granted, there are elements of speed skating training that aren't unlike that, but everything is a bit more nuanced and scientific than you'd think.

Every session on the ice focuses on a different element of the many attributes a speed skater needs. The stamina sessions will be those multi-lap affairs where we'll do two or three hundred laps at a slow, steady pace. Then, conversely, we'll have sessions that are entirely focused on speed, where we might only do six laps in the whole session, but we're doing them as fast as we possibly can.

Then there's the speed/endurance sessions and lactate tolerance sessions where we might do race distances (four or nine laps) at maximal pace. Alternatively we might do short laps with little rests in between. That covers the speed and endurance work we'd do on the ice.

Beyond that, especially in the mid-summer months, we'd focus more specifically on technique and race craft: passing, race tactics, getting used to instructions from the coach and so on, and all of this would be done at a reduced speed so that the actual details of the technique can get maximum attention.

And all of the above is only what we do on the ice. On top of all that there's the off-ice work we need to do: gym work, strength and conditioning, watt bike sessions. Basically, as an elite athlete, you've got to find a way to endure all of this. And having been good and also having been bad at various points in my career, I now know that the instances where I've been at my very best were the ones where I was willing to just ignore unbearable pain and push on throughout the many hours of tough training.

But in the background in 2017, my body was complaining. There were annoying pains and niggles here, little feelings of tightness there – all as a result of the huge force the outside (right) leg has to bear when speeding around a short track, constantly turning left-handed. And then, the faster you go – and I was going quicker every day – the more force that leg has to deal with.

As time passed, the tighter and sorer that outside leg got, to the point that I flagged the problem up at various times with my physio. In my mind I wasn't seeing it as an injury per se – but perhaps more of a precursor to one.

By the end of July – six weeks out from competition at the opening World Cup event in Budapest – it all came to a head. My leg wasn't just complaining anymore, it was bloody screaming.

My body was saying: *Elise, stop doing what you're doing...*

Various conversations were had with a number of people – including one I had with a doctor who discussed the idea of me being overtrained. Now, I know that's an expression that's thrown around quite freely in sport. But when a doctor means overtrained, they're saying it from an impartial position where they also have some kind of clinical and biological backup. It's not simply a case of someone being a bit tired and sore. They'd be basing their findings on the presence of abnormal blood levels for example.

"Elise, you're right on the edge. You're going to have to pull back, slow things down," he told me.

As much as the idea of pulling back on anything flew directly against all my competitive instincts, I told various members of my support team what the doctor had said and the gist of what came back from everyone, including Nick, was that it wasn't the time, six weeks from the World Cup, to be taking the foot off the gas by resting.

At that point I thought, *now what?*

There were really only two choices. One was to carry on with the training plan. The other was to slow down until the pain went away. But who knows how long that might have taken?

Looking back on it now, I probably should have stood up for myself by listening to my own body more and what everyone was telling me, less.

Instead, I made the decision to push on while still carrying the injury. That one is on me. But I definitely feel that I was heavily influenced into making that choice.

On reflection, I think that slowing down might have been a better preparation for competition anyway. I suspect I might have benefitted from a bit of what's called supercompensation – where an athlete trains flat-out for a finite period, then goes really easy prior to competing, with the intention that they follow this great surge in performance at the right time.

But I couldn't ever tap into that possibility because at no point did I go easy. I kept training instead, and my performance, hobbled by chronic pain, kept going down and down. The other factor to consider is that maybe that World Cup event in September didn't have to be peak me.

Let's face it: an OK World Cup performance would have sufficed in the circumstances. That's what World Cups are for. That's why there are six of them each year. At the very least I could have used them for a gentle tune-up, and that approach might have allowed me to keep peak form up my sleeve for the Olympics in PyeongChang. Ideally, I could have sat them out altogether and made sure my leg was fixed.

Obviously I'm theorising here. Would it have worked out that way if I'd backed off? I guess we'll never know.

Anyway I went to the World Cup that September in Budapest, still in pain, while the team around me was collectively saying: "Don't worry, this is an easier week." By that they meant that, with my first race on a Friday, the workload would be easier building into it than a normal training week would have been had I stayed home.

Regardless, I found nothing about that World Cup

build-up in Budapest 'easier'. Instead, at several points during the week I remember turning around to the coaching staff and saying, "Look, my leg feels like it's going to tear at any second".

Despite my protests, they were just having none of it.

The medical advice they'd been given was that I was basically imagining things – and that a tear just couldn't happen. "It's fine, it's fine," they said. They simply didn't accept that I knew my own body.

But what could I do?

In my first race, the moment I went off the line I felt the leg – specifically the TFL (a muscle that connects the hip flexor and the quadriceps) pop. It's the muscle that raises your hip as you make a turn.

At that moment I thought, *OK, well that's torn.*

Given what I'd been warning my team all week, there was a depressing degree of predictability about it all. I knew what a torn muscle felt like after all. All athletes know that feeling. I'd torn a few in the gym at various times. And sure enough, into cramp it went, sharp pains followed – and I had to finish the race in that impaired state. The problem was, while it wasn't a great race, I still won it. I almost wish I hadn't.

Everyone around me was saying, "See? You won! It's not torn after all".

I got off the ice, barely able to bear any weight. My whole leg was in spasm by this time while my team around me still said: "That didn't happen. The muscle isn't torn."

At this stage I was starting to question my own sanity – particularly when I was made to keep racing for the remainder of that weekend.

Every race, every day, the pain got worse and my movement became more limited until, when I could barely walk at all, I point-blank refused to race during the second week of the competition – "Nick, I'm just not doing it!"

Above and beyond the pain I was in, on an ethical level I was questioning why I should have been made to perform at that level with a muscle tear at all – while at the same time it being implied that I was imagining things.

I didn't even know what gas lighting was in 2017, but on reflection that's what was happening to me. That decision to keep pushing me and telling me I was imagining an injury could have ended my whole skating career, far less just my year.

A day or so later I was flown home from the Netherlands and thrown into the turmoil of multiple meetings back in Loughborough – the first of which, from memory, was with a doctor.

When I went into that examination room I entered hoping that I'd be seeing someone 'outside the programme' as it were, who didn't think I was imagining things, who had no idea about the backstory at all – just that I'd hurt myself. Perhaps subconsciously fearing an ambush, I took my mother with me for back-up.

As it turned out, one of the support team had already called back to the UK prior to my appointment and told the doctor that I just had stress-related pain. In effect, she'd been pre-warned in a, "When Elise comes to see you, this is what she'll tell you…" type of way.

Without even touching or looking at my leg, the doctor said words to the effect of: "I've heard about what's happened and it's clear that you're under a lot of stress. I'm of the belief that this is just stress-related pain."

I thought to myself, *I knew this was coming…*

What's more, I also knew that she was absolutely wrong.

The previous afternoon, I'd seen a new clinical psychologist, Vicky from *Changing Minds,* who had been helping me for a while. I'd been seeing her for periodic check-ins over a period of a few months. I always felt that she and I had a good understanding. She knew all about my various issues and where they stemmed from. She was one of the only impartial ears I've ever had. She'd told me I was doing fine, and said that I wasn't under any undue stress.

So really, from where I was standing, the only aggravation I was facing was trying to convince everybody around me that I had a genuine injury. Regardless, they wouldn't even authorise a scan on my leg because there was apparently no point.

All of a sudden, I felt trapped.

When I, the person who knew my own body better than anyone, needed listening to more than ever, I had absolutely no allies. A whole unpleasant argument ensued and eventually my mum intervened. "Please just scan her. That's the only way we'll know who is right," she said.

"We'll send her for a scan just for peace of mind, but it won't show anything," the doctor replied, reluctantly.

Four days later I went in for a scan.

A day after that I received a phone call: "You've got a muscle tear."

I was in the car with my mother at the time and instead of being distraught about just being told I had a significant muscle injury before an Olympic Games, I felt the opposite: I felt ecstatic because I was proved right! Pretty much my entire support team had doubted my sanity.

All of them had been wrong.

I was injured. But I wasn't insane.

Looking back on all of this now, I can see how, as their main medal hope, the team wanted to push me as far as I would go. That part makes sense.

However, I also know that everyone was well aware of my psychological fragility in the aftermath of Sochi, and I genuinely believe that they played on it.

The reality is that in the last few months I hadn't really had a dramatic recurrence of any of the psychological issues I'd had in the past. Up until I got injured, my life as far as training was concerned, with PyeongChang as the end goal, was going well. While I'd had my usual ups and downs off the ice and battled my self-esteem issues at various times, I always knew that I was on track from a physical perspective, so I thought I was doing OK.

But I'll confidently say that the team staff just thought, *It's Elise. Her old problems are back...* But they weren't back.

Really, the only problem I now had was them – and of course the fact that my body would probably need eight weeks of tailored rehabilitation: three weeks of nothing, then a gradual build followed by a final push back to fitness.

I actually thought it was doable. In my head, I'd already done the maths. It was September, the Olympics in PyeongChang were in February and I was sitting there, even then, confident that I could get fit in time, but only if I was allowed to do it my way. And my way meant sitting out the next World Cup meetings.

When I thought about it, I didn't even need to be at these World Cup meetings anyway, certainly not the one in Seoul in November. I had already made a final in every distance and that meant that I was effectively pre-qualified for my 'spots', as they're called, for the Olympic Games.

On paper everything was in my favour.

Then I got called into another meeting that included Nick, my strength and conditioning coach, Joe Hewitt, and the performance director, Stewart Laing. Pretty soon, it all kicked off big style. After the first couple of sentences, things started escalating.

"I don't want to go to the World Cup. I'm already qualified for the Olympics and it would be better for me to rehab," I basically said.

"If you don't go to the World Cup meeting next week in Asia, you're not going to the Olympic Games at all," Stewart Laing replied.

In my normal head, I would have taken a stand right

there and said, "OK, cool. I need to do what's best for me. And if you're telling me that I can't go to the Olympics because of that, so be it".

Because I'd been mentally tortured for a month being told I was imagining things, all while skating in pain, I was not in my normal head at all.

I stared at them, incredulous.

They stared back.

I was thinking, *OK now I'm in danger of really losing my shit here...*

"But why? I've already secured my spots. And I'm injured," I countered.

"You're being selfish. The team needs the three girls to go," I was told by Stewart.

"That's not my problem. If they can't qualify by themselves, that's not my fault," I said.

I was getting really upset. I was the main medal hope. I didn't think it was my duty to qualify other people. I knew I was being bullied. Yet there was worse to come.

"UK Sport will see you as being on a downward trajectory and won't send you to the Olympic Games..." – that was Stewart Laing's parting shot.

I couldn't believe what I was hearing. I left that meeting in a flood of tears thinking, *what can I do?*

Meanwhile, I'd had no apology from any of those who thought I was imagining my injury and no sympathy whatsoever for having been made to race with a damaged leg.

In a matter of weeks, all the faith and belief I'd built up

in my support team and plan since Sochi just evaporated. With seemingly no other option, I got on a long haul flight with the rest of the team and flew out to Asia for the next two World Cup meetings in Shanghai and then Seoul the week after.

Because of how many races there are, World Cup meetings are quite intense – and intense, in my state, was the last thing I needed while I was already carrying an injury.

These meetings are four days long, and if you make finals, you'll have skated many rounds to get there, assuming you compete in all three distances. At the end of it, you are fucking dead. It's nothing like an Olympics where you'll get rest days between rounds.

Across those two World Cup meetings, I got beaten in circumstances where I normally wouldn't have. Although I somehow managed to win the 500m final in Seoul, in the 1000m and 1500m races, people were passing me on the outside. Now *I* was the one getting dropped, and by athletes who, no disrespect intended, had no business doing so. No part of me was happy about it.

Then, to make matters worse, I was given a hard time for not being willing to skate in the relays.

Meanwhile, I was on every painkiller and the highest strength anti-inflammatories and nerve blockers possible. I could barely walk or take my blade guards off on my own and most of the time I was also walking around in a semi knocked-out state because of all the medication.

I was in agony, rolling around on the floor a lot of the

time. At night I couldn't sleep because of the pain. No way should I have been forced to compete in that physical state.

Even still, people said, "Cheer up! You came fourth in the World Cup!"

But I just thought, *I'm sorry – I'm the reigning world champion. I'm just not someone who comes fourth in the world.*

A week into the trip I'm told that I spoke to my clinical psychologist Vicky back in the UK for some advice on my rapidly escalating state of anxiety. I don't remember much about that call.

She later said to me: "I don't know who that person I spoke to on the phone was, but it wasn't Elise. That wasn't you."

As soon as I returned to the UK, I was put straight onto antidepressants called Sertraline. I didn't want to be on these tablets at that time; I'd never taken anything in my life. And from there I just did the best I could to get back into some kind of mental and physical shape.

So, on some levels, my 2018 Olympics were lost before I ever set foot in South Korea. At that point, it's sad to say that there was a part of me that didn't even want to go. I felt that I just wasn't in the place that I should have been and had worked so hard to get to. And the worst part of it was that I'd let other people dictate proceedings on my behalf.

Honestly, if I could go back to that meeting now, I'd sit there and say, "OK, well I'm not going then..." There was no way UK Sport wouldn't have sent me to those Olympics because I knew I was the world champion at the time. I'd have had no problem calling their bluff and resting for those World Cup meetings.

Despite knowing that I wasn't in the shape I wanted to be in either mentally or physically, I was well aware that when I went out to South Korea I was something of a poster girl for the British Winter Olympic team of 2018.

On one hand, although the Winter Olympics will never capture the public's attention in the same way as the summer equivalent and as much as the media focus is somewhat less, I was fine with being given this kind of high-profile billing in the UK.

Let's be honest, even I could see some of the romance in my own story. Here I was, having come all the way from being this awkward girl from Livingston, the skeleton turned multi-Olympian, to being the de-facto talisman for Team GB, and on a recovery mission from four years prior. On one hand I can't deny that it was a big deal to be going out there to PyeongChang to bring the eight-year plan we'd put in place to fruition. On the other hand, I felt a bit distracted by the weight of expectation.

Given I was the reigning world champion and had been reasonably high profile in the UK press since Rotterdam, the British public quite understandably expected me to win Olympic gold medals in PyeongChang.

Under normal circumstances, they'd have been right to do so; that level of expectation would have been entirely justified.

When I'm fit and healthy, the spotlight doesn't bother

me. But the problem was, I knew what the public didn't know: that I was neither fit nor healthy.

At least I was not looking over my shoulder every minute of every day. It had undoubtedly been a very good move on behalf of Team GB to send me out to Korea in advance back in 2014.

The upshot of all of the advanced exposure was that when I went out there in January 2018, I arrived relatively happy and relaxed in myself from a security perspective to the extent that at times it felt like I was returning not as some kind of pantomime villain, but as bit of a hero in the eyes of the Korean people.

Having said all that, as much as I had been looking forward to returning and as much as I couldn't wait to eat the Korean food and see some friends again, my first observation about PyeongChang – a ski resort 100 miles to the east of Seoul – was that it was bloody freezing compared to what we were accustomed to!

Jeezus… compared to Sochi and Vancouver, which were both bright and sunny, PyeongChang was gloomy, colourless and intensely cold.

Fittingly, on a team level, everything had changed and was more intense than at previous Olympics too – not least because our performance director Stewart Laing was much more serious and focused than his predecessor, Stuart Horsepool.

I suppose you could argue that both were very good at their job, but they had completely different ways of going about it and had wildly different personalities. Stuart was quite an interesting character and was fundamentally a guy who lived and breathed skating, very passionate, to the extent that he would have (and probably did) do anything humanly possible to get us funding and he did keep the programme going for a long, long time.

Stewart Laing was a completely different kettle of fish. He started as a physiologist in the team in around 2010 before taking over as performance director a year prior to the PyeongChang games in 2018.

For whatever reason, Stewart and I never got along. It was just one of those things. Everything was always very strained between us, and the build-up to PyeongChang had only made relations between us frostier.

Even Nick seemed more serious in PyeongChang. I didn't think that was a good look for him.

I remember one training session early on when we were on the ice at 10pm because short track and figure skating were sharing the same rink.

It was a long, tiring session and we didn't get off the ice until 11.30pm. I didn't get to bed until 2am. I was exhausted and, because of my suspect physical state, I wanted to rest the next morning because I was due to race the following evening.

"Do you know what, I think that's enough. I don't want to train in the morning. I'm going to take the morning off," I told Nick.

Historically, he'd have been fine with that. By that point

we had a certain understanding. But here in PyeongChang he wasn't having it at all.

"No you're not. I want you in, feeling your feet, feeling your blades and checking everything is ready," he replied.

I was shocked, I had to come in the next day at six in the morning and I didn't like it. Even at a World Championships, we would never train the same morning as an evening race. I'm not suggesting any of this had any direct impact on my performance. Athletes are trained to be able to perform regardless of such circumstances.

But all of this was just indicative of this new and more rigid approach that was in place by 2018. It certainly wasn't the way I would have done it, but that's how things were in PyeongChang. As always, once I'd bitched about it and got my grievances off my chest, I just got on with things like I always had.

Another issue in the background prior to PyeongChang was that I'd switched to harder blades at the beginning of 2016. To that point I'd spent my entire skating career with the same blade set up. It became one of those, "If it's not broken, why try to fix it?" type of scenarios.

Blades probably need a bit of further explanation at this point. They make a huge difference, especially on the right foot, because that's your outside foot and therefore the one that bears most pressure when you turn left.

The material used is either steel or bi-metal – half steel and half aluminium. If you're skating on a steel blade, you'll get resistance/pressure through your foot for the entire push, whereas on bi-metal, because they're softer, they tend to release and 'let go' of the force a little earlier.

The result is that on softer, bi-metal blades you tend to skate a bit 'flickier', if that makes sense? These blades are useless for sprinting. With the exception of some long-distance skaters, nobody really skates on very soft blades.

In addition to the blades themselves, the set-up of the blades needs to be considered and to that extent every speed skater likes their blades to be set up differently according to the nuances of their skating style. Some people do what's called 'skating the straights' when they're not cornering. That's when they do full pushes where the feet come off the ground. I, on the other hand, do more of a shimmy/shuffle where, after my first push, I shimmy back to the other foot rather than taking my feet off the ground.

Both of these techniques have their benefits (my shimmy arguably requires less energy because I don't have to focus on picking my feet up) but the aim in both cases is to cover the ground on the straights as quickly and as efficiently as possible.

Technique is like anything though; it goes through phases of fashion. For a while it seemed like everyone skated straights. Nowadays, more people do this shuffle of mine. As much as it's a good skill to have, I can't personally skate straights very well. If I did it in a race, I'd probably end up flat on my face.

Depending on how you skate, the blade set-up will obviously vary too. In general all blades have a certain amount of right-to-left bend, and that has to be there to allow you to turn corners. That bend can be set however you want it. Then there's the radius, which refers to the shape of the blade on the ice and the two extremes are rounder or flatter. The rounder it is allows more agility but less speed as a result, whereas flatter is the opposite.

Obviously, like in any sport, developments in skates, blades and set up are always evolving with the hope of unlocking more speed and control. But in general, as a rule, I have always skated on blades that are flatter than most other girls, the majority of whom skate quite round. So equipment is important, but then, of course, there's the nature of the ice you're skating on to consider.

*****

To backtrack for a moment, 100 days before the Olympics, the whole short track team had been out to Asia, first to Shanghai and then to Korea in advance of the Olympics.

There were a number of reasons for this trip apart from the two World Cup meetings, and the primary one was to use it as a bit of rehearsal for when we arrived early the next year, whereby we could work out how quickly the jetlag wore off and, most importantly, see and feel the ice arena in PyeongChang where the competition would take place.

Ice, like skating equipment, is a complex thing and it's rarely the same in each venue. Broadly, you'll get dirty or clean ice. Clean is fine, dirty (caused by tiny particles that you can't even see) will strip your blade edges and make you fall over for no apparent reason. Then there's soft ice, hard ice and brittle ice – all of which vary according to the relative temperature of the ice and the air.

If the air is too warm, as it usually is at the National Centre in Nottingham, the ice will be too soft. Brittle ice is where both temperatures are too cold. Then there's fast ice and slow ice, all depending on these various environmental interactions or, as is the case in Salt Lake City, where they use some kind of fancy ionized water to clean the ice. There the ice is essentially artificially altered to be very fast all the time.

As a speed skater, you are absolutely aware of every conceivable ice condition and there are very few places in the world where there's consistently good ice. The moment you get on the ice, you know exactly what you're skating on. If it's brittle, as soon as you start skating you'll hear that tell-tale sound of tiny cracks forming beneath your feet. On soft ice your edges don't have the same grip.

So, the first thing I noticed about the Gangneung Ice Arena was the abnormally cold temperature and, by extension, the condition of the ice – which was hard and fast on first inspection. This fact obviously informed the ongoing conversations Nick and I had been having about what blades would be best for me.

In recent years, blades had become a bit of an odyssey for me. As I'd got better and as I searched for even more of an edge in competitive terms, I also started tinkering with them and my set-up much more than I probably should have.

By the end of the 2016 season, because my sprinting was getting faster, Nick and I had discussed a few options that we thought might maximise this raw speed even more, and in the end we had decided to try a blade that, while it was definitely meant to be faster, was also much more rigid, unforgiving and frankly quite uncomfortable to skate on.

While I was fit and well, this blade was absolutely fine. It was indeed demonstrably faster than my previous set-up. My World Championship gold medals in 2017 had confirmed that. But as soon as I got the leg injury on the lead-in to PyeongChang, the weakness and pain in my leg effectively negated the benefit of those new blades.

In addition to being uncomfortable to begin with, the hard blades meant that I became very static in my skating. In training in the lead up to PyeongChang, I was constantly turning round to Nick and saying, "I just don't think I can skate on these blades".

"It's too close to the games to change," he said. "And anyway, they are faster," he added. I just had to stick with them.

Equipment issues aside, on the hard ice of PyeongChang I did well in the 500m to start with. I was clearly one of the strongest girls there and because there's less impact on an injured leg in a shorter race, my physical shortcomings weren't really tested in the early heats. My leg was definitely sore, but not as sore as it might have been. Indeed, I was in good enough form to break the Olympic record twice in the early rounds, albeit that the Korean girl Choi Min-jeong bettered my time twice later.

In the semi-final, Canada's Kim Boutin beat me off the start, which I expected given she was the fastest starter in the world at the time. But with two laps to go, I passed her quite easily. As I did so, she skated into me and we both flew out wide whereupon we got passed by the Dutch girl, Yara van Kerkhof, who eventually won.

Meanwhile, Kim knocked the Chinese girl off the track while she was trying to cut back in to rejoin the race.

In the end, Yara won, I was second, Kim was third and the Chinese girl was fourth (she was later disqualified despite having done nothing wrong) because Kim had skated into her.

Initially, I was standing thinking, *great! Kim's not going to the final – the only person that can beat me off the start!*

At the same time I was also considering that I'd probably end up drawing Lane 4 in the final, because our semi-final had so many crashes and the other semi was therefore quicker.

Even though I knew that Yara and Arianna would await me in that final, I only saw a gold or silver medal on the horizon for me.

But wait, weird shit was about to go down again.

With two girls from each semi going into the final, Kim got advanced to the final having finished in third place, by the same American referee that I'd had all the issues with dating back to Sochi. My problem was that, according to the letter of the law, you could not be advanced from third place because, technically, you were not in a qualifying position. Despite that, Kim still got advanced!

I was thinking, *what the actual living hell is going on here?*

As bizarre as it all was, it wasn't helpful for me to dwell on it. I had a final to compete in 10 minutes later. And even though when I went into it from Lane 3, I had more or less decided in advance that I knew that I'd be fourth off the start given that Kim, although she was drawn outside me, would be quicker off the start and would therefore block my route into second place.

In my head I was thinking, *it's fine, I've only got to pick one person up and I've got a medal. Then I can go for the win in the 1000m.*

The immediate build-up to an Olympic final is undoubtedly a strange place to be. By this point in my career I'd been in countless races and I'd won many medals, some of them gold. I wouldn't say I'd become blasé about it, but World Cup events were a bit more relaxed by virtue of the fact that there's so many of them each year. World Championships always felt huge and up until 2018, they had probably meant every bit as much to me as the Olympics.

Now that I'd won two World Championship gold medals in 2017, the Olympics seemed the most important goal given that I had never won an Olympic medal of any colour at either Vancouver or Sochi, for all kinds of different reasons.

For that reason I would be lying if I said that the pressure of my first Olympic final in 2018 didn't carry an awful lot of weight.

Especially in the 500m, the excitement before a race is heightened by the fact that everyone knows how vital the start is. So, while I don't normally worry too much about races beforehand, in order to anticipate the start as best you can, you want to arrive at an Olympic 500m feeling the way you would if you'd had way too much coffee – and for me that's a combination of edgy, chatty, every nerve and muscle ready to react, to *anticipate*.

Before you even get to the start, you warm up for 20 minutes and then go and go and sit in the heat-box with your fellow finalists. Before an Olympic final, a heat-box feels like someone has sucked all the oxygen out for your inconvenience. It's quiet; everyone's so focused. I don't like it. There's nothing going on for the 15 minutes that they hold you. That's where you sit, think about the race, and in my case, feel short of breath.

Sitting in the heat-box in 2018 before the 500m, as experienced as I was and as much as I always backed myself, I was realistic enough to know that I probably had no chance of winning the race I was about to skate in.

The sad truth was that, once I got injured before the games, instead of focusing on all three distances equally, I had to narrow my focus down to one distance. That distance was the 1000m, and therefore anything I achieved in the other two were always going to be a bonus.

EIGHT

HONEST

PRE-GAMES PREPARATIONS ASIDE, I SUPPOSE if I'd been drawn in Lane 1 in that 500m, I might have felt a little differently.

If I'd been in 1 and Kim in 2, as much as I knew she'd have beaten me off the start, I'd only ever have to pass her – which I thought I could do. The other two girls would never even be in the race.

Beyond that, I couldn't help thinking that, had I arrived at the games in perfect shape with an uninterrupted preparation, I even think I would have had a chance to win it from lanes 2 or 3. The previous year I'd medalled in almost every 500m I skated in, no matter where I'd been drawn. I'd won a fair number of them too.

But as it stood in PyeongChang, with my injury and my focus more on the 1000m, I was in a very different place than I'd been in at the Worlds in 2017 to the extent that, honestly, sitting in the heat-box I was thinking, *I'll just be happy to medal at all here…*

The biggest relief of all in an important 500m is when the race actually starts.

In that moment, you're no longer thinking; you're only doing – and it's all happening on instinct like when, half asleep, you make the same breakfast every day of the week. All you hear is your heartbeat and the air rushing past your head.

I went off the start and as I'd predicted, I found myself in fourth place and was pretty happy with that given my leg didn't allow me to start as well as normal. At that point, all I was thinking was, *I just need to pick off one person and I've got a medal here…* Then, as I held back and then accelerated away from the Dutch girl Yara to drop her, I saw a crash happening in front of me and thought, *OK, someone's getting DQ'd for that.*

Then I passed Kim, as I had predicted I would, but as I did so she bloody hit me again. In that instant I swear I was thinking, *you shouldn't even be in this race, yet here you are barging into me again!*

As I wobbled after the impact, I actually thought I could stay on my feet. And because I was sure that one of the ones in front was going to get disqualified, I was even thinking, *silver medal!* However, I hadn't bargained for Yara, who, having been miles off the back just a second or two earlier, came through from absolutely nowhere and skated through my hand on the ice as I was getting back into my lean.

People watching on TV might say, "Well, why didn't you just keep skating?"

But believe me, when you're travelling at 30mph on ice and then someone skates into your hand, no matter how strong you are, you're going out the side. It has happened to me twice in my career. There's no way you can stay on your feet.

And that's what happened. I went careering into the barrier. I'm certain that if she hadn't hit my hand, I would have finished in third and picked up a bronze medal at the very least, depending on what happened with the disqualification in front of me.

The worst part of all of this was that there was no disqualification anyway! The referee called nothing whatsoever after the race. One girl skated into me and another skated through me, and nothing happened. I couldn't believe it.

Worse than that, you've got absolutely no recourse to question decisions at the time. You can't say anything.

"What the hell just happened?" I asked Nick.

"You clearly went past her and she just skated into you," Nick said.

He couldn't understand it either.

Even though I knew I wasn't going to win and was probably heading for third place, out of all the Olympic disappointments, that's the most annoying medal that I've lost because I did everything against the odds. My leg was in total agony the whole time; I was doing everything I could to just finish the lap. And just before the incident happened, with half a lap to go, I was thinking, *I've done it!* I knew that Yara was miles behind me.

Sadly, this ruling was only part of a developing pattern. I mentioned what happened to the Chinese girl – that she was disqualified from the semi-final when she'd done absolutely nothing wrong.

Understandably, China believed that Canadian athletes were being favoured at their skaters' expense and so after the Olympics, because of this and their general dissatisfaction with the quality and consistency of ISU refereeing, they decided to refuse to hold events in China. Technically we should have had a fifth World Cup event in the year after the Olympics but it didn't happen because the Chinese refused to host it.

In general I've always felt that rules are a real weakness in our sport because, relatively speaking, it's such a new sport and therefore the rules are evolving in real time. Because of that, they're hard enough for us to learn, far less anyone watching at home who might know little or nothing about short track.

When I went to my first Olympics in Vancouver 2010, I remember thinking that the rules were OK. Even since then, many have already changed and in my view, that has made the sport not only more difficult to skate in, but also a much less digestible spectacle for viewers. Some of the rules are just so incredibly vague, not to mention being subject to whatever interpretation a referee wants to go with in the moment. For example, one rule, 'entry to the corner', as it stands as of now, says that in order for a passing move to be legal, you have to be past the leading skater by the entry into the corner.

In theory, that's fine. I can see how it would make sense to have to be in front. But in practice, there is no standard entry point to the corner. Not only that, every skater in the world enters a corner at a different point, on a different line and from a different place on the track. On that basis, you may as well scrap that rule altogether, because all you'll get are decisions based only on a referee's interpretation of a rule, not the rule itself.

The other rule that's so tough to apply is what's called 'change of direction'. Here, a referee is looking at whether a skater moves off a true line and causes interference with another skater in the race. And they assess this by looking at a front-facing camera to establish which skater is deviating most off that straight line.

Again, in theory, this rule and the means of applying it, is reasonable enough. But in practice, it's never that straightforward because sometimes the reason a person deviates from a straight line is because someone else has skated into them. Some referees in that instance will say, simply, "She changed direction", regardless of the *reason* for that change of direction. That skater will be penalised, whereas the skater who collided with them to cause them to move off a line, won't be.

On many occasions I've thought about our sport,

particularly when I try to watch it from an outsider's perspective. I've tried to imagine I've never skated in a race, and when I do, the overriding thought I have is that if I didn't know what it physically feels like to be in a short track race even I would sit probably sit there and say, "Err, what just happened? I'm not sure who caused that incident. I don't understand this sport".

But because I have been in many races and know how quickly events happen within races, I can look at decisions and say, "I understand why that's been called that way it has. But it's still the wrong decision as per the rules".

When you extend my theory to the public, who not only have never been in a short track race but also might never have seen one, they've got zero chance of understanding what the hell is going on half the time. From that perspective, I can totally see how someone could be sitting there in front of the TV in the evening with a drink and some crisps, watching the Olympics saying, "Oh, there's that Elise Christie, just falling over again..."

In the real world, most of the public just aren't going to have the inclination to know all the rules. They just want to see a race and (hopefully) see me win. But, regardless of the public's view on things (and that's a much bigger conversation related to the idea of growing the sport), I do have to take the time to understand the scope of the rules in my sport.

Success and failure, gold or no medal at all; it all hinges not just on my ability as a skater, but also on my knowing what the limits of the rules are and, by extension, what any one of us can or cannot get away with in the white-hot atmosphere of an Olympic final. And in that 500m final in PyeongChang I know they broke the rules. I was skated through twice and nothing happened – that was wrong.

Then, as if that wasn't bad enough, there shouldn't have been five skaters in that final in the first place. The rules clearly state that you can't be advanced from a non-qualifying position. It's black and white. If Kim hadn't been in it, fucking hell I'd have been in second position off the start and that might have made all the difference.

When I got off the ice after the 500m, Nick and Shaolin were there and their view was that I shouldn't immediately go into the press when I was still in an agitated state.

"Don't go in, yet," Nick said.

"I'm going in because I'm going to be honest," I replied.

I wasn't going to go in there and be honest in the sense that I was going to blurt out all the problems I'd had in the previous few weeks and months. I had to keep that under wraps. I still had two distances left. But I did want to show my disappointment about what I felt was yet another terrible decision that had gone against me at an Olympic Games.

Inevitably, after the 500m, I indeed did get a few of those, "There she goes, another Olympics and here's Elise Christie at it again – falling on her arse in a final," type comments online.

At the same time, I also received a lot of nice comments and positive messages from people who had evidently become super-fans, and who could see I was clearly on the wrong end of another bad call.

As a general rule, I went to PyeongChang wanting to keep a low profile so I tried to stay off social media as much as I could. That was intentional, and was me simply trying to not get distracted or sucked into pointless negativity. I tried to keep any activity limited to Instagram pictures, but at the same time I turned my notifications off and arranged for Rory, my agent, to only send me select and positive stuff from kids etc. The rest he managed from back in England, and he did so to preserve my sanity.

After the 500m went Pete Tong, my leg was really sore and I knew that the next two distances were only going to be even tougher on it.

"You know what, I don't know if I want to skate the 1500m," I told Nick.

For different reasons, I was thinking in the same way as the Korean girl had been in Sochi. I thought that if I skipped the 1500m, I'd be giving myself the chance to recover a little, added to the fact that I'd always known that the 1000m was going to offer me a better chance of winning a medal.

Nick disagreed.

"No, but your chances of winning a medal are better if you skate in all the distances," he said.

I could see his logic to a degree, albeit that I wasn't in the shape required to skate in all distances at peak form. But it wasn't as if I *couldn't* medal in the 1500m. After all,

I was world champion at the time having won the gold medal in Rotterdam a year earlier while becoming the first British woman to ever do so.

So I ended up agreeing to just do the 1500m and in the first round I dropped everyone. Nobody was near me. When I got off the ice after the first round I was sitting there crying.

"I don't think I can keep getting round the corners," I said to Nick.

At every corner, I felt like I was going to fall because my knee was wobbling. I was terrified it would just give in altogether and cause me a serious injury.

"I think it's your blades," Nick said.

Initially I believed he might have been right. I actually hoped it was my blades because at least I could do something about them.

But deep down, given what I was feeling, I knew it wasn't the blades and that really it was my leg. As strong and fit as I felt aerobically, the leg just felt so weak in its capacity to hold my body up under the extreme pressure of cornering at speed.

To make things even harder, I drew a super-tough semi-final – way harder than the other one. It was basically like an Olympic final if you swapped one person out. At the start I felt two emotions. Firstly, I was apprehensive because I was weak, sore and anxious. But more than that I was thinking, *well, OK – but I'll just blast everyone anyway!*

I messed up the tactics very slightly in that semi-final,

and I did that because I didn't make a move when I should have. The reason I didn't was that the Korean girl Choi, the most likely winner of the gold medal, was trying to skate me out of the race. She's the kind of girl that, if she doesn't want you in the final with her because she sees you as a threat, she'll try and knock you in one of the earlier rounds.

My initial plan was to get to the front and to try and dictate matters by picking up speed and doing some defensive lines. Even still, I accepted that Choi might pass me if I was doing most of the leading, but it wouldn't have mattered if she'd beaten me in that round and I knew she raced differently in finals anyway.

But every time I tried to make a move, Choi kept jumping out in front of me to stop me from making one. I started getting nervous, mainly because of my knee, and in the end I waited way too long to make a decisive effort to put myself in a strong position to challenge.

Eventually, with only three of us left in the race – the three strongest in the whole competition – when I went to go round the outside at the end to pass the Chinese girl Li Jinyu to go into second place, she seemed to jump and took me out with her.

The thing I remember most about this sequence of events is that, on some level, I knew it was coming. At the corner before the incident, it was clear to everybody that I was going to pass the Chinese girl imminently.

That everybody included the Chinese coach, who I

clearly heard shouting something to his athlete before she jumped into mo.

As I slid into the barrier I was in the most pain I'd ever experienced in my life. My foot – on the same leg as the injury that had plagued me prior to the games – was swelling by the second inside my fibreglass skating boot. I can't describe how sore it was, and I've felt some pain in my time. Meanwhile, the medical people were trying to put me on a stretcher as a precautionary measure in the event that I had sustained a neck injury.

"No! Take my boot off!" I cried.

"Oh but what about your neck?" they said.

"There's nothing wrong with my neck! Take my skate off!"

I was taken to hospital and while the X rays weren't clear, they could see enough to suggest that there wasn't massive structural damage. Nothing appeared to be broken. That news gave me a glimmer of hope.

The next morning they woke me at 4am to go for another scan. While the MRI clearly showed there was some ligament and tendon impairment, the extent of it was hard to establish because everything was still so swollen.

They never re-scanned it. Instead, they sent me back to the village and at that point I assumed my Olympics were over and that I'd be sent home to England imminently. I thought there was no chance that they'd even consider letting me race in the 1000m.

Immediately after the race, the Chinese coach apologised

to Nick. That afternoon, the Chinese girl came and found me to apologise also. She didn't specifically say *why* she was apologising, but as a weird kind of peace offering, she handed me some pin badges.

"I'm sorry. My coach told me to do it," she said.

Meanwhile, I was in a bloody support boot and on crutches, my Olympics seemingly ruined, thinking, *I don't want your bloody pin badges thanks!*

Before the race, Shaolin had said, "Watch out for the Chinese girls". He'd seen races on YouTube where Chinese girls can clearly be heard telling each other to take someone out. But when the race started, I forgot all of that.

So, I suppose it was no shock to me that they might have been perfectly prepared to sacrifice one of their own team to eliminate me. Those kinds of team tactics are absolutely commonplace in short track today – particularly from the Koreans and the Chinese who play on the fact that it's hard for everyone else to understand the orders as they're being issued. We don't understand what they're saying, and somebody watching at home would have no idea that such dark arts are even taking place. But dodgy stuff happens all the time, believe me.

Instructions from the side are, of course, an intrinsic element of the sport.

As much as we're encouraged to skate for ourselves and not for a team, Nick does the same for me to some extent and I need his input to cut through the noise in my head.

Obviously, in an Olympic final I'm thinking a million

different things about the race, especially in the longer distances. Who's in front, who's behind me, can I go inside, can I go outside, do I need to make a move – all of this is a constant dialogue and it's changing all the time, second by second.

Meanwhile, Nick is watching everything from the side, and having been an elite athlete himself he knows exactly what I should be doing and where I should be at any given moment. He sees everything I see, albeit through a wider lens.

But his instructions are intentionally unambiguous. Whenever he needs me to do something in a race, he just shouts, "Elise!" That's my sole trigger. And because of our hours, years, of working together, I always know what it is he's wanting me to do and when.

The problem is, other coaches latched onto this habit after a while – to the point that there was a Korean coach who would also shout, "Elise!" during races, just to confuse me. On the first few occasions it happened, for a second I'd have to look around to see who was doing it. Some people will do anything to get an edge.

In addition to communication from coaches, there's often more said by athletes during races than you'd ever know from watching on TV – especially from the Chinese and Koreans, who are always talking amongst themselves because they know that nobody else will know what they're saying.

Other stuff you'll hear is just the occasional rude word

or the odd "get out of my way" when a bump looks likely to happen. I'm not averse to a bit of that myself, depending on what kind of mood I'm in. I've certainly given it the occasional, "Don't fucking touch me…" too, when things have got a bit heated.

In general I'm always quite chatty, but only in the heat-box before I get on the ice. I like to say things to wind people up and to do that you've got to know them a bit to understand their habits and what makes them tick.

A favourite of mine is a bit of false flattery – that really gets to some people. I might say something like, "Seriously, if you don't bump anyone in this race, you've got a real chance of coming second". That gets a few of them thinking and wondering whether I'm really playing them a compliment or just winding them up.

Some girls don't say anything and don't like any chat at all and hate when I talk. I remember getting told to fuck off by a rival skater, Suzanne Schulting from Holland, after we'd been called back after a false start once.

The funny part about it was that I wasn't even talking to her. In the moment, I just thought the circumstances of the false start were funny and a couple of the other girls started talking too. But Suzanne obviously didn't like being taken out of her racing zone and she told me so in no uncertain terms.

Anyway, I digress…

I wasn't sent home to England after the 1500m in PyeongChang. I can't even remember what I was thinking about it all as I sat in the apartment in the village.

At that point there were two clear days ahead of the 1000m heats. But to be cleared to compete at all, I had to be able to show that I could somewhat skate on the morning of those heats. Meanwhile, there I still was, in a support boot and on crutches, with just 48 hours to rest. The two didn't really add up. It wasn't looking great.

"We're not going to make a decision now. You just do everything you can and then you make the decision based on how it feels," Nick and the physios said.

For the whole next day, I switched back and forth between whichever recovery methods I could tolerate most. I'd do a quick spin on the bike, which was obviously hard given I was in a boot. Then I'd ice it, then compression, then more ice and so on. I was going round and round with whatever I could. I only ever paused to eat or sleep.

Throughout all of this, I was hardly allowed out of the village. Nobody wanted the media to see me and my food was brought to my room. I wasn't allowed to see Shaolin because nobody from foreign teams was allowed in our apartment anyway.

As I recall I wasn't even allowed to see my mum – who was the person I most wanted to see while I was in that stressed state. The only person I had apart from Nick was Charlotte, but she was no bloody use to me because she just sat there crying all the time!

I suppose we were all living through my situation. As well as being my best friend and roommate at the village for the games, Charlotte had been through the previous four years with me as part of the inner circle that included Nick and Shaolin.

And to that point, I'd never truly been properly injured at a major competition although before we even went to the Olympics, given the issues I'd had in the build-up, we had obviously discussed possible worst-case scenarios.

"What will you do if you break down from injury in competition?" someone said.

"I don't have a bloody clue," I replied.

And, now that it had happened, I genuinely didn't have a clue.

I mean, what can you do in a situation like that? It wasn't like a World Cup where there are always more races and other days. At a World Cup you might even shrug such a situation off. I've often told people that when it's *not* the Olympics, short track skating is so much fun. We race, we laugh, we fall over and we maybe get a bit frustrated now and again. But ultimately we're out there enjoying what we're doing. And there are six World Cup meetings each year.

But this *was* the Olympic Games, where four years of your life get boiled down to just one race. That's no fun at all. And when you're in a situation like I was, you either try to salvage something from the wreckage, or you go home. There's nothing in between.

In the end we did everything we possibly could, and even then I could still hardly walk on the morning of the heats.

I was still in the support boot; I showed up at the ice and attempted to warm up on a bike while still wearing it. It's just as well that I had really old skates because I even had to take the tongue out of one of them to get my foot in at all. Had they been any newer than eight years old, I'd have never got my foot in.

Looking back, all of this seems so ridiculous now. Again, had it not been the Olympics, not a chance in hell would I have gone anywhere near an ice rink.

I didn't even tighten the skate up properly. I could barely get a skate on my foot. I just closed the Velcro fastener and got on the ice.

At that point, as I mentioned, I'd switched over to skating with the hardest blade in the world on the right foot. But within about two seconds I realised I was going to have to swap it for the softest blade on the planet if I was going to be able to skate at all. We switched over. I basically went on there again with a kid's blade that wasn't even set up properly and started hobbling around the ice like a beginner.

"If you can't tolerate this, there's no way you can race," Nick said.

But, the upside of the softer blade was that I couldn't feel anything through my foot, so it didn't matter how the hell blade was set up!

Somehow I forced myself through the pain and made it work enough to prove that I could race, helped by the fact that I was also on every painkiller that was legally available to me at that time. When I turned up for racing that night, everyone was gobsmacked.

"What the hell are you doing?" people said.

Most people hadn't even seen me for two days since the injury happened. The press had no idea what had been going on in the background.

Yet, come race time, there I was, sitting in the heat-box where I needed people to help me put my skates on and take my blade guards off. It was all a bit surreal to say the least.

I was trying not to think about very much of anything, but the competitor in me, as impaired as I clearly was, couldn't help but consider my race in the context that, had I been going into it under normal circumstances, I'd have most likely dropped everyone. I really thought the 1000m was my best distance, in the same way as Usain Bolt, as amazing as he is at the 200m, would probably consider the 100m to be his better distance.

Of course I'd be lying if I didn't also mention that I knew that there was quite a high likelihood of me not being able to race competitively at all. But I'm nothing if not an optimist, and so I went into that 1000m heat with a hope that everything would be OK rather than much in the way of real belief.

So I thought, *well you know what, if I can get through this, I'll have another day and a half of recovery until the next round.*

If I'm being totally honest, it was some of the messages

my agents had screen-grabbed for me from supportive kids that really got me on the ice that night at all.

I've always considered kids to be the most innocent of beings, temporarily uncorrupted by the shitty realities of life. They've never judged me. I've never once had a kid tell me I'm a failure. And the reason they haven't, I guess, is because they know nothing of the wider issues that surround me in the adult world – the trolling and the general hate.

Instead, they just see me as this girl to look up to, and to that extent they just want to encourage me and believe in me and I guess I always just want to repay that faith. If I just gave up when there was a way to keep going, what message would I have been sending them?

As a result, I couldn't have lived with myself if I'd just bailed because it was a bit sore in PyeongChang. I felt a real sense of responsibility. Hurt or not, I still wanted to inspire people – even if I knew full well that it wasn't going to be the real me out there on the ice that night. And it wasn't. When I look back at the footage, I barely recognised myself. My skating was hilarious.

Anyway, when I went off the start, I knew these kids and the rest of the world would be watching.

Then a girl stood on my ankle.

Remember when I said that the pain I felt when I crashed into the barrier in the 1500m two days earlier was the most extreme pain I've ever felt? Yeah, well I lied!

When that girl stood on my ankle, the imaginary pain

meter in my head went past 10 and just kept going. I can't even describe it. People thought I was crying, and granted I had a solid track record of doing so in public by then. But I wasn't. My eyes were watering with sheer pain as I sat on the barrier thinking, *I've got no chance now...*

"You need to get off the ice," the referee said, talking directly in my ear.

I just ignored him for a bit but he kept persisting. "I need a minute to think," I eventually told him.

I somehow stood myself up and thought, *I can't put any weight through this.*

At the same time, as I clung to the barrier in total agony, I was thinking about all those kids watching me at home again. Had it been any other situation, I promise you I'd have hobbled off the ice and called it quits that night. But, again, I just couldn't do it. I just didn't want to let those kids down by quitting. I wanted to show them that, whatever life throws at you, you can always prevail.

I, however, was the only one thinking like that.

"Elise, this is too much. You need to get off now," my physio was saying, while at the same time I could hear Nick shouting me over.

"Elise... get off," the referee said.

I skated over to Nick and he fiddled around with my blade for a bit, loosened it and then tightened it up again. I knew he was only trying to buy me time.

"Get off, now. You are not safe to skate," the referee then told me again, quite forcefully at this point.

"It's not your decision!" I told him.

"You're not safe," he repeated.

"I'm *going* to skate," I told him.

"OK, if you start again and it turns out you're not safe, you must go and stand in the middle," I was told.

He'd at least given me a chance.

I went back to the start and lined up again. Had I been at my peak and strong, in an Olympic 1000m final the plan would have been to get out in front and lead to stay out of trouble.

Because of my stamina and strength, while I might not have won, I'd have been confident of medalling.

There's no way three skaters would have got past me.

But this wasn't even close to my peak. And because of the pain in my ankle, when I'd been hoping to get out in front and do some leading, I got left at the start instead. They dropped me by about four blocks and I then had to use a lot of energy to catch them.

Skating on sheer bloody determination and pride, I caught up, passed one and thought, *oh, that's good. I'll do the other one now.* I passed her, she passed me back then I passed her yet again to finish in second place and qualify. I was bloody buzzing.

I couldn't believe everything that had just happened. I was chuffed to qualify, but more than anything I'd shown those kids watching back home that you should never give up because, no matter what, you could still do it.

Even still, Nick had to carry me off the ice because I was

in so much pain. We sat in the cool-down area where I was taking my skates off before I went in to talk to the press.

Then Shaolin walked in.

"Erm, you've got a yellow card," he said.

Well, to that point I'd never had a yellow card in my entire career. Yellow cards are for people who do intentionally dirty things like the one the Chinese girl did to me under instruction in the 1500m. Or they're also given for two penalties.

But I wasn't known as a dirty skater. Clumsy? Sometimes. But I was never dirty. I never intentionally skated into anyone, grabbed people or dragged them down from behind. If anything I've always tried to skate as cleanly as possible. If I can get out in front and stay out of trouble, I will.

Well, they had given it to me for two penalties. I couldn't believe it.

"I've literally just dragged myself up and done this, and he's given me a bloody yellow card. What for?" I said.

Everyone was gobsmacked, including the girls that I'd passed in the race.

I started crying.

Then I thought, *sod this, I'll go to the media and then I'll go and get a McDonald's.*

Standing there in the media zone, every time I started an interview, I opened my mouth but no words came out. I just kept choking up and crying.

As hard as I tried, I just couldn't talk about it – I'm sure everyone has seen the TV footage. It was the first time

I'd ever been in a position where I couldn't talk. I'm not ashamed of having shown my emotions like that. In fact I don't understand people who can't show their emotions publicly.

In the moment, I was just sharing how I was feeling. Four years of work had amounted to nothing. Like Sochi before it, PyeongChang had gone tits up in a very public fashion and there was absolutely nothing I could do to fix it.

What you were seeing in that moment was simply the cumulative disappointment about all of that being laid bare for all to see. As much as some people might not understand how anyone could care about their sport so much that they'd cry on TV – that's why I was crying. I cared so much.

On reflection, I was probably going through shock, which is obviously the first stage that immediately follows trauma.

But on further reflection, it probably helped that I cried so much that I couldn't speak because I simply hadn't processed what had just happened sufficiently to be able to talk about it in any meaningful way anyway. The only thing I was sure of as I sat in front of the press was that my 2018 Olympics were over.

It feels like a mere afterthought to mention that I got the yellow cards for what the referee thought were two dirty passes. That was his opinion, and in his capacity as an official that's his right and his duty to enforce the rules.

But my opinion is that the referee didn't want me to

start that race in the first place because he didn't think I was safe to skate. Why else would he say the things he said when he told me to get off the ice or to stand in the middle?

The ironic part is that every other referee in the competition came up to me to congratulate me on what I did that night. I had other skaters coming up to me and saying, "You're my hero" and, "I'm so proud of you for getting on in the shape you were in".

Even the video referee didn't agree with the calls. But there's nothing you can do in that situation. The chief referee's decisions are final. But I personally thought he was a liability – a bit like I was when I found myself hobbling around on crutches again after I finally got through the media zone!

Appropriately, my Olympics in PyeongChang ended with me being carried onto the ice by Shaolin after Hungary won the gold medal in the relay a couple of days later.

Officially, I shouldn't even have been there. If you're not racing, you're not allowed next to the barrier. But one of the Korean officials must have felt sorry for me and let me stand and watch the race through the barrier while the Hungarians won gold.

Afterwards, Shaolin and his brother were understandably going mental about winning and came over to me to celebrate. I remember making a mental note of the fact that I was the first person he came to.

As disappointed as I was for myself, I was unreservedly pleased for him. In that moment, that meant something.

And then when he carried me onto the ice and I stood with his team for the picture, it felt good for those few seconds. That was, at least, an upbeat end to my second disastrous Olympics in the space of four years.

As we did every year, we had an end-of-season review after the Olympics in PyeongChang. Inevitably, in specific relation to me, there was a lot to go over given not only my performance at the games themselves, but also the build-up to them in the weeks and months prior.

Obviously there were mistakes made and I've been very open about saying that I felt I was being railroaded into something that I wasn't able to do, and my opinion is that Team GB were thinking about the corporate side of things to the exclusion of the wellbeing of the athlete.

For obvious reasons, they'd wanted me in PyeongChang. As the reigning, overall world champion and someone who brought a bit of much-needed box-office to a minority sport, I was unquestionably the most marketable member of that Team GB at the 2018 Winter Olympics, not to mention one of our main medal hopes.

However, all of that marketability and box office amounts to nothing if the athlete, the *human,* behind the marketing image isn't fit and happy. And that's pretty much what I felt so aggrieved about. I wasn't fit and happy at all, but they pushed me anyway. They used me.

Now, I totally get that, because it's a team, there were a number of people and, by extension, lots of opinions combining to arrive at some of these pre-games decisions on my behalf. But at the end of it all, I came out of the whole process trusting only one of those team members, and that was Joe Hewitt, the physical preparation coach.

Joe was the only person in the whole support network who behaved as if he believed what I'd been saying. And while he couldn't actually make major decisions or pull me out of anything, he at least had made every effort to find solutions that made things better than they might have been.

"Let's get your glutes firing and your hamstrings firing so that the injured muscle has to work less," he'd say.

Granted, it wasn't a perfect solution. The damage was long done. But at least he had done the best he could to improve the situation, which is more than anyone else did.

So, as unpalatable as this might be for some others on the team to read this, Joe was the only member of the team I trusted in the immediate aftermath of PyeongChang.

And as hard as it is to say it, given we'd worked together for almost 13 years, Nick let me down too in the lead up to the 2018 Olympics. And he knows it. I know that because we've discussed it since and there were certainly some tears shed on his side about it all. He knew he hung me out to dry to a certain extent.

I don't, however, sit here today and blame Nick, even though I did blame him publicly in that end-of-season review. At the time I was prodded and probed by everyone around the table to voice my opinions. They wouldn't stop pushing so eventually I bloody flipped and just blamed

Nick for everything. And with retrospect, the only reason I did that was because I was so hurt and disappointed and Nick was the one I'd trusted most.

The reality is that, if there was anyone to specifically point the blame at, it was Stewart Laing. It was he who didn't believe what I was saying. It was he who ultimately made all the decisions. But I didn't do that at the time and there have been many times since where I've wished I had.

More than anyone, I blame *myself* for allowing myself to be bullied at all. But an apology from some of the others on the support team certainly would have been nice. Given everything I'd been through, I thought that was the least I deserved.

To add insult to injury, because I was unable to go to the World Championships after the Olympics in 2018, UK Sport told me that I'd be dropping from 'A Card' back down to 'B Card' because I didn't have a top-three finish at a World Championships (or an Olympics, obviously).

On one hand, I suppose the policy is fair enough. Just because I'd been on the top level of funding since 2013 on the back of World Championship medals in every season between 2013 and 2016, and just because I was the world champion in 2017, didn't mean that the rules didn't apply to me. I was OK with that, as brutal a policy as it is.

However, I thought that there were extenuating circumstances in 2018. Yes, the Olympics had been a disaster and I'd missed out on top-three places for a variety of bizarre reasons, but I'd gone there injured and under pressure from both Team GB and UK Sport. I thought that, in those circumstances, I deserved a bit of funding latitude given that I wasn't able to go to the World Championships, far less medal at them, because of the same injury.

Basically, when it came to the funding review, I begged them. Given everything that had happened, to drop down a funding level would have been unthinkable. After a lot of back and forth, they reluctantly agreed to compromise and extend the 'A Card' funding level until September 2018 but really, given that I'd been injured, they shouldn't have taken my 'A Card' funding off me at all. However, being UK Sport, they just did what they wanted anyway.

NINE

THE FIRST CUT

PRIOR TO THE OLYMPICS IN 2018, I HAD NEVER self-harmed properly.

Truthfully though, I had only toyed with the idea on a very superficial level when things got too much for me at various times, but I'd never actually acted on the impulses and caused myself actual physical damage.

With hindsight, I think that, as much as things went wrong in my life from time to time: bullying, rape, a house fire, disappointments at Olympic Games, injury and so on, there was always something in my life – skating – that I was able to use as an outlet, a pressure release valve is perhaps a better description, for the emotions that I might have been feeling.

As I've said before, skating became my salvation early on in my life. I loved it and still do. To skate fast gave me actual joy. But more than anything, whenever I felt anxious, upset or whatever, I always knew that I could call upon my superhero alter ego: Elise Christie the world champion, the fastest woman on Earth, and just get on the ice and blast everyone away.

On one hand, having a reliable fall-back persona is a great thing. It empowers you when you're playing that role and you are motivated to perpetuate it because you know how important it is in terms of maintaining your emotional balance.

But equally, on the flipside, it can be a crutch in the sense that you can't help occasionally thinking, *what if I didn't have my skating abilities to prop up my self-esteem?*

Now, obviously I'm not stupid. I know that this skating career will end one day, as much as I don't want it to. But on many occasions in my career – at World Championships, at European Championships, at World Cups and even during some of my less than perfect Olympic Games experiences – I have often caught myself in the moment wanting to just freeze time and hold onto the feeling of crossing the line as a medal winner, or even how it feels to be a top-level competitor at all, forever.

At times, in my capacity as that timid girl who'd transitioned from Scotland, a country that wasn't exactly renowned for sporting greatness, to becoming a world champion and sitting among other sporting greats at the BBC Sports Personality Of The Year in 2017, I even remember thinking, *this is too good to be true!*

And from there I'd try and savour every single moment

in the knowledge that, of course, it couldn't last forever. But there comes a moment when your luck runs out and your well of resilience simply dries up. And when I got back from PyeongChang in the spring of 2018, I was bang there.

In the first instance I was so disappointed in myself because I'd allowed other people to dictate the outcome of my Olympic dream. On top of that, there were also a lot of historical and unresolved issues in my life that I'd not dealt with and I'd used skating as an excuse to kick those issues down the road, to be dealt with at some unspecified later date.

But eventually, I reached the point in the road where all the things I'd previously kicked down it lay there in front of me like some kind of impassable roadblock. As hard as I tried to fend off all of the negative events that had somehow come to a head in 2018, I just couldn't do it. As the year progressed, I was losing control and I knew it. The problem was, very few others outside of my immediate circle had a clue what was really going on with me,

The great thing about an Olympic sport is that no matter what happens, while you're young enough, you always know that there will be another Olympic Games in four years.

Furthermore, in the unique case of our sport, the racing calendar is always the same in the sense that the build-up to each Olympic Games is a set cycle that is more or less the same from year to year. World Cups, Europeans, Worlds, short break in the spring, start again in April, train all summer, compete again in late September. That schedule is always there – and with that comes a sense of comfort in that each meeting is always offering something new to aim at and with each race comes a chance to achieve elation.

Now though, because of my injury rehab, Nick and I had agreed that I wasn't going to skate competitively until the World Cup races in Turin in February 2019. All being well, the plan was for me to be back on the ice in September, and then to maybe compete at a couple of the World Cup meetings at the end of the year so I could be part of the team and perhaps skate in a relay or two.

2018 started to look like this barren wasteland where I wouldn't be racing at all. All I'd be doing would be trying desperately to get my ankle back into a shape where I'd be able to race again.

The timing could hardly have been worse. Between 2015 and 2018, for all that there had been continuous emotional anguish playing out in the background of my life, I'd enjoyed arguably my most productive years on the ice. I'd won many medals, eight of them gold, broken world records and become Britain's first ever short track world champion. I'd even been voted Sunday Times Sportswoman of The Year in 2017.

Whichever way you looked at it, the eight-year plan had worked to a large degree, even if the ultimate goal – Olympic medals – had still eluded me in the end.

The long route to another Olympic, light years away in Beijing in 2022 in reality, looked arduous and that wasn't helped by the fact that around May 2018 I heard our programme had lost its lottery funding.

When I heard this news, I admit I was pretty negative about it all, even though I hugely appreciated that I had kept own my funding. As far as the overall programme was concerned, I just thought, *how is this even going to work going forward?*

Suddenly, I didn't have the daily distraction of going in and following a rigid schedule – tied to competing down the road – but also the programme as a whole was in disarray. I kept thinking, *what will even be there when I get back?*

Meanwhile, I couldn't even think about racing and being unbeatable. Instead, I had to concentrate on fixing my leg and, beyond that, rebuilding my whole self.

Unfortunately, I was in no mental shape to do any of this. I had no fall-back persona and I was out of routine. To compensate, I started medicating properly.

In the run-up to PyeongChang I'd had enough conversations with the clinical psychologist, Vicky, to know that I was already pretty close to being depressed in late 2017, prior to the Olympics.

The darkly hilarious part of it all is that, at that time, Team GB thought I was losing it but in reality it was them and their attitude to me that was pushing me to lose it by not listening to me when I kept telling them there was something wrong!

Christ, I knew my own body; I knew something wasn't right. But to be continually told not only that I was imagining things but also that I should keep pushing it – and all this by the very people who were meant to be there to support me – was a significant part of the reason why I started slipping further in the first place.

To avert this, I was prescribed what was just meant to be a temporary course of antidepressants to take the edge off things and for a while they did that.

I began to feel less and less – no crushing sadness but, equally, little in the way of joy. As a rule, I don't necessarily think that's a healthy position for an elite athlete to be in. Depending on how my skating went, I always swung between absolute elation and tears. And the reason I did either was only because I cared so much.

But it had got to a point where I had to suppress these extremes. I'd gone from being the most confident short track speed skater on the planet in March 2017 – the world champion. At that time, I was certain I'd medal at the Olympics. I was superb at all three distances. But then, just a few months later, my self-belief was circling the drain on the back of the injury fiasco, and along with it any realistic chance of medals in PyeongChang.

So the point where I just didn't want to feel at all had to come. But now, here I was a few months later and even antidepressants couldn't keep me straight. They just weren't cutting it for me, no pun intended.

I was a broken athlete.

By summer of 2018 I was really losing it on a grand scale. In addition to bursting into tears all the time about the most stupid things, I started drinking a lot more than I ever had. The irony of that, dating back to my mother's worst fears in Livingston when I was growing up, was not in any way lost on me.

The mad part of it is that I hadn't drunk at all in the two and a half years prior to PyeongChang. I actively avoided alcohol because it just wasn't part of the game plan and I could never handle it very well. Now it was very much part of my plan, and I couldn't get enough of its numbing effect.

I wouldn't say I was ever an alcoholic during this time. It's actually very difficult for an elite athlete to be an alcoholic; the two mindsets can't coexist easily. So while it wasn't a clinical state of dependency I was dealing with, it was bad enough. I was bingeing on the weekends and getting seriously off my face and that's enough to suggest that I wasn't exactly in an elite athlete's state of mind during this period.

It was only later that I realised that instead of being any kind of solution, alcohol was just another form of spiral in itself. When you're depressed and on medication you're not even meant to drink alcohol in the first place. And then when you drink you get even more depressed and so you just think, *well, I'll just drink more...*

And from there, there's only one outcome. Down and down you go. And I could definitely feel myself sinking.

Obviously, while all this was going on, Shaolin's and my relationship was edging closer to the precipice. As much as we cared for each other and our relationship had been strong despite the challenges of long distance at times, there came a point where, as much as he probably loved me, I was no longer the same 'me' that I was when we met.

For that reason, I genuinely think he simply wasn't equipped to handle everything that this new, super-damaged version of Elise was putting him through. And that, I suppose, wasn't his fault. I'm not sure anybody could have handled the lunatic I'd become by June and July 2018. Even on the occasions when I was with Nick, despite our mutual level of understanding, he couldn't deal with me or relate to me in any normal way.

I'd be bloody screaming, bursting into tears and throwing stuff like milkshakes at his head – sometimes all at the same time. It must have been obvious to him that something major was amiss.

"What is going on, Elise?" Nick would say.

"I don't know. I feel like I can't control myself," I would tell him.

That, to be honest, was an understatement. I was far beyond the point of not knowing if I could hold it together. And people forget that Shaolin wasn't an experienced, grown adult coach like Nick was. He was much younger and had his own elite career to think about, far less trying to prop up mine while I was totally unravelling in front of him on a daily basis.

On reflection, I think my cutting, my self-harming – whatever you want to call it – was the last straw for Shaolin.

He simply couldn't relate to it on any level and the reason he probably couldn't is that nobody can unless they're in the kind of mental place I was in.

As irrational as cutting your own body with a sharp blade until it bleeds clearly is, in the early experimentation stage in 2018 it wasn't as if I didn't know what I was doing.

On the contrary, I knew *exactly* what I was doing and everything about it was extremely clinical and controlled: I was using the instant shock of stinging pain as a means to disperse or replace whatever emotional pain I was feeling at that moment. It was really that simple.

The first time it happened was a few days before Shaolin and I broke up. And clearly I think I did it because I knew a break-up was on the cards. I was preparing myself for the emotional pain that I knew was going to come, and in a sense, by cutting myself in his company, I was hastening it.

Predictably, he just freaked out when he saw what I'd done. What was strange was that he didn't actually say anything as the fresh blood was streaming down my hand and wrist from a three-inch cut on my forearm. But the look on his face told its own story. It said, "This is too much".

People since have often asked about the specifics, "How did you actually do it?" and other similar questions, but really it wasn't that complicated.

I had just got a knife and did a couple of trial cuts to my arm and in that moment I suspect it felt like that first moment when a heroin addict feels when they first inject heroin into a vein. There was a sudden rush, in my case a flood of searing pain, and then that was followed by a period of blissful relief from whatever mental anguish had caused me to pick up a blade in that particular instance.

At the outset, on that first occasion, I was pleasantly surprised to discover that by cutting myself I could buy a good couple of hours of relief, and that the purchase, unlike drugs, cost absolutely no money.

I could bask for a while, and float off into this weird netherworld of therapeutic pain. And then, all I had to do when the relief wore off was cover the wound with a plaster and roll my sleeve down to conceal the evidence. Job done. That was the end of it.

That was enough – at least until the next time.

But like drugs, alcohol or any addictive habit, enough is never really enough. As I did more of it, I started realising that the period of relief was shortening. Where I was once buying myself three hours, those three became two, and then one.

The only thing I could do to stay in that emotionally detached state was to keep cutting myself more and more often.

I even began to experiment a little with technique in the sense that I found ways to cut differently (and deeper, if need be) to get a better, longer lasting effect.

My arms became a right mess, and once Shaolin left, that mess became my lonely secret for a while because, unlike some instances of self-harm, none of what I was doing was a cry for help in an exhibitionist sense. It wasn't like I was walking down the street with my arms uncovered as if to say, *look at me, I'm cutting myself to bits. Help!*

Now, there's absolutely nothing wrong with that approach. Sometimes drawing other people's attention to a harmful habit is the only thing that pulls someone out of the shit. That's when a cry for help fulfils its purpose.

But at this point I didn't even want to be pulled out of the emotional mire I was in. I didn't want anyone to see. As irrational as it was, cutting was my only coping mechanism at that time and I needed it badly for myself and myself only. Telling someone else would have only increased the chances of an intervention and, by extension, somebody taking my only coping mechanism away. That was unthinkable. So nobody, not my mother, not Nick or even Charlotte knew what I was doing.

The bizarre thing about all of this is that, as much as I felt I was always in total control of my self-harm, I absolutely hated myself for doing it. I thought it was so fucking weak, something I never saw myself as being. I didn't even like the trait in other people.

If you'd asked me in, say, 2013, what I thought about cutting I'd have probably said, "I literally do not understand how anyone could cut him or herself. I just don't get it".

But I guess that everyone who doesn't self-harm feels exactly the same way.

One of such people was Shaolin – who finally left me for good in late July 2018.

I feel differently nowadays about it all but at the time I

was just so mad at him because he was literally all I had left at a time when I was at my absolute lowest.

However, he'd made his mind up that he just couldn't cope with me and he just cut off contact all very suddenly at a time when, because we'd had our funding pulled in the UK, we'd been actually discussing me going to Hungary with him to live and train for the next four years.

As crazy as it might sound, and as off the rails as I was, it hadn't been too long previously that we'd reached a separate position whereby we had to make a decision whether the relationship had a permanent future. When he left, everything, including any suggestion that I might move to Hungary full time, obviously went straight out the window.

I just thought, *how could he do this to me?*

But because of his age and the fact that he had no experience of either being in the place I was in emotionally or even having experience of anyone else going through it, I think I was just too much responsibility for him at that time. He probably saw no option other than to leave, cut ties totally, and get on with his life.

And this he did, in the coldest way imaginable. Not surprisingly, much has been made since about the fact that he told me we were splitting up by text message. But the truth is, I just told someone in the press what had happened. I simply said, "I got dumped over text" and from there a juicy line like that got blown out of all proportion, as these things often do.

Just to be clear, at no point was I suggesting that the

mechanism of being dumped in that way ruined my life or implied that he had no manners. That wasn't the point. It was just a throwaway statement of fact said without filter in an interview, which is how I am by nature. But in the world of social media there's no doubt that these things can get magnified far beyond how they were meant.

And boy did this get blown up in the UK tabloids…

Consequently, in the weeks after we split up, Shaolin was unhappy about this particular comment and some of the other things that came out in the British press about our break-up. I didn't say half of the things that the press claimed I had, but by that point everything he read about us in the British was pissing him off.

In my opinion, given when the split took place, I think Shaolin was quite naïve to think that he wouldn't get painted as the villain in the UK press. It was only because it happened shortly after my very public tribulations at the Olympics that anyone even cared. Had the break-up happened a year later, I doubt anyone would have been that interested.

In the weeks that followed, after an initial period of no contact at all where he deleted every picture of us together off his social media in the first 24 hours, Shaolin and I started communicating again on some level.

It wasn't a remotely romantic conversation; I don't really know what you'd call it. He'd just randomly send me updates about what he'd been up to and vice versa, pictures and so on. Feelings of some kind were clearly still there on both sides.

It's not for me to say of course but I got the impression at that time that he was struggling with the fact we were apart. As much as he couldn't cope, I don't think he wanted to leave me anymore than I *wanted* to cut myself or I *wanted* to be a totally unhinged lunatic every day.

I started realising that as absolutely rubbish as it was that he couldn't stand by me through anything, he just couldn't do it. His attitude in these awkward calls in the autumn of 2018 made me see things from his perspective in the sense that I understood that, as much as I'd lost him, he'd also lost me – the person he loved and cared about.

It really felt like he at least missed what we once had, and that understanding really opened my eyes to viewpoints other than the narrow minded and self-centred, *how could he fucking leave me?* angle that I'd been clinging to up until then.

As the autumn wore on, in parallel, I did finally talk to Nick about what was happening in my life and he was, in his own way, very sympathetic.

I don't think I intended to talk to him, but when he noticed the scars on my arm when I took my tracksuit off one day training, his attention couldn't *not* be drawn to the marks of shame that I'd tried so hard to conceal. From memory I think he said something along the lines of, "Elise, is there something I need to know?"

"Well…" I said.

And we started talking.

Although I don't think I really acknowledged it over the years, Nick always was a kind of father figure to me on some level. When I look back to the early days before, say, Vancouver in 2010, Nick had to pretty much fulfil that role to the whole 20-plus person group in general. He'd drive us places and pick Charlotte and I up in various parts of Nottingham if we got lost and a host of other little jobs like that. It was a very different culture in those days. You probably can't do a lot of these things nowadays. Nowadays, athletes aren't even allowed in coach's cars.

After Vancouver, Nick and I went into what I consider to be the second phase of our coach/athlete relationship whereby he knew all about my abilities and my willingness to train every day as if each session was my last. And then, because of my insistence that we had to put a plan in place if I was to be the best and win medals, I actually think that proposal of mine woke Nick up and made him think, *this girl is very serious about what she wants. I need to be working with her.*

Consequently, the era that followed, all the way up until the 2018 Olympics, was more of a mature, person-to-person relationship. And as much as Nick and I battled each other at various times about all kinds of things, we always had that certain unspoken understanding between us that only occurs when two strong-minded, competitive people know that they share some of the same traits.

We'd even worked through our problems since the PyeongChang fiasco where I'd blamed him and lost trust in him. In the absence of any other ideas, I had just thought, *I can't change what happened now. Let's move on from all that...*

Then the worst thing happened. Nick was made redundant, and he was given only four days' notice as far as I understood it.

I don't know what the back-story was. One suggestion I heard was that his superiors felt he had had every opportunity to win a medal for the team but had failed, and that, I suppose, was true. Part of me even felt guilty about my part in that.

There were also suggestions that there were some personal issues between him and performance director Stewart Laing, but I never had any knowledge of those personal ins and outs. I was never aware of what went on behind closed doors within the running of the programme.

All I know was that it definitely wasn't Nick's decision to leave, and that he was being replaced in the role of head coach by a South Korean coach and former short track skater called Seung-jae Lee.

Talk about upheaval! As much as Shaolin leaving me was devastating, Nick's departure was absolutely horrendous in the context of my already chaotic world.

At that point, in late November 2018, I literally had nobody I was prepared to talk to and, worse still, Nick's redundancy meant any plans that he and I had previously made regarding scheduling were now subject to change, even though he tried to assure me that everything would still be fine.

And change they did.

"We want you to race at the Europeans," Seung-jae said

at some point in November after we returned from one of the World Cup events in Calgary, where I'd taken part in the relay to test my leg and to see where I was fitness-wise.

"Well, I'm not ready to race at the Europeans. The plan has always been to come back properly at the Worlds and the funding people at UK Sport are fine with that," I said.

"I want you to skate at the Europeans in Dordrecht on January 11th", Elise," he repeated.

Let's just say that being told what to do by a new coach, and for that instruction to be wildly different to the target I'd been working towards for months, did not sit well with me.

I went in that emotional/irrational place that I can get into very quickly, and at that moment I went there because I felt like I was being bullied all over again – and at a time when I'd barely got over the anger I'd been feeling about being ignored and pushed to keep training prior to PyeongChang.

For the first time I felt totally trapped by my sport – a sport that had just lost its lottery funding at that. As I thought about the idea of being sent to the Europeans in January against my will when I clearly wasn't fit to race, I also considered whether I wanted to be a skater at all.

TEN

THE DEEPEST CUT

BY DECEMBER 28TH 2018, I HAD REACHED breaking point. No matter how I tried to rationalise everything in my already scrambled brain, I just couldn't see a way to could escape all the problems that had piled on top of me, one after the other. I had this feeling in my chest that just wouldn't let up.

Shaolin had gone, Nick was gone and I was in a state of extreme financial distress that had been building for years. As a result of some rash spending at various times, I'd accumulated around £10,000 in debt.

That combination was a bad enough place to be in but on top of all that, I was also an elite athlete recovering from a serious injury while being told by a new coach that I had to compete at major championships with just two weeks notice. It was all too much. I'd just had enough.

Christ, I was still very damaged after PyeongChang and

as much as I was on tablets, they clearly weren't working well enough. For a long time everything had been shoved under the rug. In that moment I said to myself, *everything is coming out now...*

That night – it was a weekend – I had my friend Brett staying at my house. He knew how much I was struggling and I guess he thought it best if I wasn't on my own. At around midnight, I went upstairs and sat on the bed in my room.

As I did so, unlike all the other times I'd cut myself, I wasn't thinking logically at all. While I held the razor blade against my lower left wrist and pushed harder, much harder than I'd ever done previously, all I could think about was that I just wanted the way I'd been feeling for so long to go away.

For a period of time that I can't recall, I think I left my body and hung suspended in the air just below the ceiling of my bedroom, staring down at a 28-year-old girl that I didn't recognise, slumped on the bed.

I could see the blood running, and I could also identify the two sides of the incision she'd made hanging open enough to expose what looked like the white pulp of human flesh and all the various tendons and arteries that went with it. As horrendous as it was, I was so zoned out that I was totally indifferent to this image.

Then, in an instant, I was back on the bed as myself and now I was the opposite of indifferent.

I was *panicking* – shouting at the top of my voice.

"Brett! Help! I don't want to die!" I yelled down the stairs.

Now that I was back in my rational self, I wanted help, and before long Brett had me in his car, driving me to the hospital. He'd already called an ambulance and they'd said, "We can't get there quickly. Can you drive her here?"

Brett's a good friend, but he's also very squeamish and not at all good about seeing blood in the quantity that I was losing it while sitting in his passenger seat. I'm not squeamish at all; I'm a lot more pragmatic about such things – always facts based as I've said so many times.

"Yeah so…" I said, "Can you look at this and tell me if you think what I'm seeing is an artery," I continued.

As I showed him the cut close up, I could see the colour draining from Brett's face.

"Oh for fuck sake, Elise," he said, barely able to look at it.

By that time I think I'd worked out on my own that it probably wasn't my artery I was seeing after all, and that I'd cut through a tendon instead. Along the way I phoned ahead to the hospital and asked them what I should do and they told me to wrap it in a wet towel and to hold my arm high above my head to slow down the flow of blood.

By the time we reached the hospital, I guess my body's blood-clotting mechanisms had kicked in and done their job. The cut was still wide open, exposing the various bits within, but instead of pouring blood, things had calmed to more akin to a sticky, steady ooze.

When I walked into A & E, the hospital staff recognised

me immediately and took me straight through the public waiting area, which was full of the usual weekend drink-related casualties. They sat me down in a private room where I could be on my own until they could dress the wound and bandage me up.

"You're going to be fine. You've just cut the tendon," they told me.

OK so I'd cut the tendon, but typically of me, I cut one that serves absolutely no purpose. I was lucky in that respect I suppose.

The saddest part of the story is that I might as well have told them I was just another of those weekend drinking casualties we'd just walked past in the waiting area. Instead of telling them what had actually happened, I told them I'd been out, got drunk and had fallen on a broken bottle.

I doubt they even bought that suspect story of mine. Given the location and nature of the wound, my explanation wasn't especially credible with hindsight. I suspect they knew exactly what had happened, that I'd done this to myself.

But at that moment I felt so ashamed and so very angry with myself. I didn't want to tell anyone what I'd done. And I knew that for confidentiality reasons they couldn't force me to say either. I left with the wound sutured and bandaged up, and when I walked out of the hospital door I promised myself that I'd never do it again.

The next day I went around to Nick's house to tell him what had happened. As I mentioned, he was the only person who had any understanding of where my head was at but I don't think even he had expected me to cut myself to the extent that I had. I also had to tell my physio part of the story because I knew that he'd be responsible for changing my bandages.

My new coach, Seung-jae, I told nothing. I just didn't feel like I knew him well enough to start divulging my deepest emotional secrets so early in our relationship. Whenever he saw my bandages, which inevitably he did given I was back training, I just told him that I'd cut my arm on something sharp as I walked past.

*****

Nowadays, I look back on all of these events with a lot more perspective. People ask me questions all the time like, "Did you want to kill yourself?" and the sad truth is that it's just not that straightforward. But what I can say is that, in that moment, I don't think I was sitting there thinking, *I want my life to be over.*

As ridiculous as it might sound, I don't think I was rational enough to think like that. The logical part of my brain had been temporarily hijacked because I'd been feeling the way I had for so long.

But seeing what I'd done to myself, I suppose was the shock I needed to bring my logical side back, in the same way as you hear of people who survive having jumped off a bridge. As they're standing on the edge, they're irrational enough to jump from a great height. But then, after having jumped, their logical brain kicks in again as they're falling to the ground, and they immediately think, *hold on, I don't want to die.*

I don't think my situation was any different to that, although obviously I'm aware that in both instances there are people who do die when they cut themselves or jump off a bridge, and sadly, we'll never know what they were actually thinking.

But for me, as much as I didn't want to continue living as I had been, in the precise moment that the blade went in deep, I really don't think I wanted to die. I had never, ever previously considered suicide by overdose or any other means. I just wasn't 'me' that night, and I simply wasn't self-aware for those few moments to pull back from the brink.

To that extent, I consider that night in December 2018 to be a very different thing from what I call my 'normal' self-harm attempts – where I'd always been overtly aware of what I was doing. Really, the only commonality was that they both involved me cutting myself with a razor blade.

For some reason I called Shaolin not long after the bad cutting incident happened. He didn't answer. After a few hours I sent him a message and said, "Look, can you please answer?"

He picked up.

"I've cut myself real bad this time," I told him.

From there I just started crying, telling him how sorry I was, telling him how much things needed to change. I even told him about our funding issues. I let it all pour out. I'm not exactly sure what it was that I expected from him. But it didn't matter because he didn't really say anything in response at all.

For fuck's sake, I wasn't even talking to him like a girlfriend talking to a boyfriend in that moment. I was *desperate*, and was only looking to him on a basic human-on-human level – like a road crash survivor, trapped in their car until the ambulance arrives, might welcome being talked to by a passer-by that stumbled upon the scene. The Shaolin I knew was always looking after family, making sure friends were OK and I don't doubt that on some level he still is like that. From that perspective, despite our differences, I just wanted to feel that he cared.

I, however, got none of that empathy on that phone call. And I knew at that moment that anything he and I had ever had was gone.

As he hung on the phone saying nothing whatsoever, I thought, *you're not even the same person.*

In some ways coming to terms with this fact made things a lot easier for me. As time passed, I went from being furious to irritated, to indifferent and finally to a state of enlightenment where I was able to look back on our relationship and identify some glaring signposts that I'd missed in the past because my judgement had been obscured by a combination of my feelings for him and my own emotional turmoil.

The truth of the matter is that when Shaolin and I first

met, he was just an up and coming, talented skater and I was a minor celebrity who'd attracted a degree of notoriety on the back of my drastic Sochi misfortunes. Also, as I mentioned, having been skating at a high level for almost 10 years prior to meeting him, there was a lot I could offer Shaolin outside the normal trappings of a boyfriend and girlfriend relationship.

None of this is to suggest that what Shaolin and I had for a long while wasn't special, loving and genuine – it definitely was. However, when he got a little famous in his own right, I think, in retrospect, he changed and I just didn't pay enough attention to notice that at the time.

The first warning sign I thought about when I considered things later was in PyeongChang when I was sitting in the apartment at 11.30pm that night after the ankle injury in the 1500m left my Olympic dream in shreds.

Charlotte was in tears; even Nick was distraught. As I said before, my Olympic journey wasn't just mine; there were others involved too and one of them was Shaolin.

I was sitting there in agony, wondering whether I'd be able to get on the ice again thinking, *what a waste of my life this all is.*

That day Shaolin had raced too, taken a few people out in the final and got himself disqualified. At the time I hadn't seen it, I still haven't, but that night, knowing what I was going through, he called me and said something to the effect of, "Well, I've had a shit day. But at least I'm not injured!"

I couldn't believe what I was hearing. It felt so insensitive, selfish and uncaring. Even my ex-boyfriend Jack, with whom I'd endured that horrendous break-up, had messaged me to say, "Elise, I'm so sorry. I hope you're OK".

Despite the bitter nature of our split, Jack has always cared about me so much and vice versa. But for me, to get the opposite reaction from Shaolin, a person I actually thought I had a better relationship with than Jack, was shocking when I think back on it.

At that point though, I made no fuss about it at all. On one level I think I took that position because, as much as I was going through, I wanted to put him first because he still had more races, whereas my competing in the 1000m was still highly questionable. And even if I did somehow manage to race, I had little or no expectation about being able to do well whereas he had a legit chance to win medals.

On another level, I think I convinced myself in that moment that he hadn't really meant what he said and that everything was actually OK. I now know that I did that simply because sometimes it's easier to let something slide, despite alarm bells, and to just hope it goes away.

At the time I just thought, *don't make a big deal out of this right now, Elise...*

But, in relationships, I don't think incidents of that kind ever go away. They need resolving, or else the relationship falls apart. Having stewed on it for a while, I brought the incident up again about a month after the games. Shaolin flew off the handle.

"You're making out like I didn't support you," he said.

"You're the one that's supposed to care the most!" I said.

"You've got this upside down," I went on. "Even with my injury, I was on that barrier cheering for you. I was the one supporting you while you won an Olympic gold medal. Do you think many other elite athletes could have done what I did?"

As I was saying all this, I did think back to the World Championships in 2017 where I'd won everything and Shaolin was there, cheering me on. He was so happy for me and seeing me so successful seemed to excite him. Then, a year later, when I wasn't winning, it felt like being with me didn't hold the same appeal to him, to the extent that I now think he was only ever with me for my status.

With the benefit of hindsight, I think there's part of me that knew Shaolin and I had serious issues at that point after PyeongChang. But because of what I was going through, I just didn't want to say anything for fear of pushing him away.

In isolation, some would argue that the incident in PyeongChang was just a one-off and therefore not reason enough to question the whole worth of a relationship. However, after we split up, a few people came to me and told me stories that really gave me pause to think about things a bit more.

People, even including members of the public, told me that when I was on TV in PyeongChang and clearly injured, Shaolin was seen smiling. Even I've seen pictures where I was crying and he was, as people said, smiling.

It was all so strange for me, and all I could think was, *how did I not see this?*

*****

After that night when I called Shaolin to tell him about the bad cutting event, he never once thought to check in on me and to see how I was. In fact, when I showed up at the European Championships a couple of weeks later, he had his new girlfriend with him in the changing room that I was also in.

Let me be clear, it wasn't that I cared that he had a new girlfriend already per se – that part didn't matter. What bothered me most was the fact that, knowing I'd cut my wrist open and had been in hospital a couple of weeks earlier, he didn't even consider how his actions might impact on me given it was my first competition back.

I thought, *really? Wow. I don't need you at all.*

Thereafter we barely spoke, even when we found ourselves together at the same race meeting. It was just about civil, but in the most indifferent way imaginable.

Having been each other's everything; we just had no interest in each other. He never once asked how I was doing.

Looking back on this whole situation, I've often thought how strange it is how two people could be so invested in each other and so into helping each other towards the common goal of an Olympics, only for everything to just vanish to a point where it's as if they never knew each other at all.

Obviously I know I'm not the first to be in a situation like that; these things happen all the time and people split up after 40 years together and having had children together. But it's still bizarre how it can all go so bad.

Without question, it was the hardest relationship I've ever had to get over because I didn't just lose Shaolin; I also lost the final component of a support team that I'd been with for several vital years of my life.

There was a lot of loss for me to take, including some of Shaolin's family with whom I'd become very close. But regardless, I'm comfortable enough with myself to know that, no matter how much a situation might sour me, I just don't need people like the Shaolin of now in my life on any kind of level, even as a friend.

Today, as much as I don't particularly respect what Shaolin is nowadays, I am able to look back on what we once had with absolute respect. I'm able to separate those two things because they *are* separate – in a 'that was then, this is now' type of way. When you can do that, I believe you're growing as a person.

ELEVEN

GOING PUBLIC

IN THE SPRING OF 2019, HAVING GONE TO the European Championships in Dordrecht under duress, I somehow managed to do reasonably OK despite all the turmoil that had preceded it, winning a silver in the 1500m and a bronze in the 1000m, having led until two laps out.

I put all of this purely down to natural ability. With only a couple of relays in November and December under my belt, it was extremely gratifying to acknowledge that I was still able to show up after almost a year off the ice and get into finals.

On paper, it wasn't bad at all. But really I was far from OK, and that wasn't helped by the fact that Seung-jae and I had absolutely no common understanding or communication whatsoever. Let me be clear: it wasn't as if we disliked each other at all; we were always fine. But as a coach to athlete relationship, Seung-jae and I never really worked.

None of that was his fault – bless him. He just didn't know me well enough to understand the many idiosyncrasies that Nick had had more than 10 years to figure out, and even we'd had to work at it through some ups and downs.

Dr Steve Peters's book *The Chimp Paradox*, which came out in 2012, had been a significant key to the unlocking of Nick and my coach/athlete relationship and, as it turned out, Steve Peters worked closely with our own team sports psychologist, Dr Mike Rotherham, and he spent a lot of time talking us through the book's messages as a group.

In the initial years of working under Nick, one of the things I struggled with most was taking any form of criticism. And the reason for that was clearly because, given my experiences at school where I started criticising myself because of other people's opinions, I had never really shaken that trait off. As much as I was motivated, whenever I was criticised, even constructively, I had a tendency to get irrational and then go off into an emotional place where it was difficult to get through to me.

The paradox taught me that the reason for this response was mostly tied to my ego. For example, at low moments, when I wasn't on form or something wasn't going well, I'd mouth off to protect my ego, or I'd avoid doing something I'm shit bad at, again because of my ego. When Nick criticised me, my response was usually driven by my ego. All of this was part of the reason that Nick and I battled at times.

In the early years, I just wasn't self aware enough to

understand any of these subconscious responses. As much as he was considerably older, I'm not even sure Nick was either. But once we both understood the tenets of *The Chimp Paradox*, we both grew, both as individuals and as a coach/athlete team.

Consequently, towards the end of our relationship, Nick and I had reached a point whereby we both understood exactly why the other did what they did. We didn't need to battle. There was a synergy there and that allowed Nick to instinctively know how to handle me when things weren't going so well.

Unfortunately, Seung-jae and I never had the luxury of spending enough time or effort together to understand each other in this way. We were strangers, in every sense, thrown together by circumstances and with no shared experiences to work from. This made talking difficult – and the communication vacuum between us was never better exemplified by the fact that, by the time I got to the World Championships in Bulgaria in early March via two World Cup meetings in Turin and Dresden in February, I was completely overtrained. As much as everyone knows that you've got to be on the ice to get race fit, we'd somehow managed to get the balance so horribly wrong.

Other than making the 'B' final in the 500m, I really didn't skate very well at all in Sofia. I wasn't in any way surprised, Physically I was battered; I spent most days in an ice bath desperately trying to recover in whatever way I could. Meanwhile, Seung-jae, whose approach to coaching

The National Ice Centre in Nottingham has helped produce some great talent. Here I am pictured with, left to right, Jack Whelbourne, Jon Eley, Charlotte Gilmartin and Richard Shoebridge

...was all smiles at a press conference ahead of the 2014 Winter Olympics in Sochi. The smile would not last long once the Games had begun...

Above, Arianna Fontana of Italy, myself and Park Seung-Hi of South Korea fall during the Short Track 500m at the 2014 Winter Olympics in Sochi and, below, reality hits home that my 500m gold medal dream is over

hi continued to bring moments of pain, both physical and emotional. I crashed out of the 1000m semi-
al and was also disqualified after the judges ruled that I had made contact with Chinese skater Li Jianrou

If looks could kill... My face says it all after the 1000m fall and disqualification

Not my usual Sunday night! Being interviewed by presenter Clare Balding at the BBC Sports Personality of the Year 2017 event at the Liverpool Echo Arena

That rare evening of glamour, left, at the Sports Personality was very enjoyable and, right, yet another Team GB photoshoot as I prepare for the 2018 Winter Olympics in PyeongChang

Myself and, left to right, Kathryn Thomson, Charlotte Gilmartin, Joshua Cheetham and Farrell Treacy goof around at Heathrow Airport on our way to PyeongChang

Mum cheering me on in PyeongChang. She has always been my biggest supporter and the sacrifices she made for us as kids will never be forgotten

Below, I win my Short Track 500m quarter-final ahead of Canada's Kim Boutin (right) in second and Hungary's Andrea Keszler

Different Games, same pain. I crash out of the Short Track 500m final

...eeded medical treatment after ...ashing out of the Short Track ...00m semi-final and I could not ...op the tears from flowing

...ey build us tough in Livingston! Despite being on crutches and in a lot of pain, I manage a smile at the ...na and, right, I was determined to enjoy the Closing Ceremony. Olympics are too rare, and too special, to ...squeeze the most out of them

I am Elise Christie. I am still here, still competing, still aiming for Olympic success. Still alive

was much more intuitive and a lot less fact-based than Nick's, was at his wit's end already.

"I don't know why you're feeling like this and I don't know how to fix it," he basically said. It was a shambles.

The 2019 World Championships were the worst of my life, and who knew back then they'd be the last World Championships for some time.

*****

The off-season of 2019 was so pivotal in my life. Having had an awful year in the aftermath of PyeongChang, with all the issues that I've described, I'd hit rock bottom in December 2018.

However, having survived that major turning point in my life, I got back on the ice and proved to myself and everyone else that, more than anything, I was a survivor. No matter what I went through, I was resilient. I understood that more than anything in 2019.

Now, it's a powerful enough moment when you do something to save yourself, but by April I was starting to look at everything I'd been through from a completely different perspective.

Instead of internalising and making everything this grim personal struggle shrouded in secrecy, suddenly I felt the need to make it less about me and more about other people; people that might be in a similar position to the one I found myself in that night in December 2018.

On April 29th 2019, having got off the antidepressants I'd been on for almost two years, I decided to go public. I should say first, as an aside, that I'm extremely impulsive when it comes to social media and always have been. What you see on my Instagram is generally a reflection of exactly what I'm thinking or feeling at any given moment.

Whenever I feel like posting a picture of my dogs or cats, I do. Equally, if I feel the burning need to post random song lyrics that meant something to me at that exact moment, I do that too. Random selfies with cryptic messages to accompany them? Yup. Serious agency shots of me skating at major championships? Absolutely, they'll be there too from time to time, as well as desperate appeals to building experts in the Nottingham area to help me fix the bodged half-finished extension at my house.

Nothing is off limits. My profile is basically a random stream of consciousness with nobody directing it or overseeing 'content' other than my own emotional state. At no point have I ever discussed or 'cleared' anything with anyone like agents or UK Sport before I posted it.

Consequently, you never really know what you're going to get with me and I like that about social media. So when I posted a long statement about my own battles with mental health on April 29th 2019, I'm pretty certain it was like a bolt out of the blue for most people, including a lot of people who thought they knew me well.

The funny thing about that post was that I composed it, posted it and then had to go to an event to present an award that evening. When I got up on stage, everyone started clapping and cheering more than I had expected; I wasn't immediately sure why. I always feel so self-conscious in those situations,

Then I realised.

The Instagram post had gone far and wide. And what I said had obviously struck a serious chord with people in a positive way. It was so refreshing to have the UK internet blow up in a heart-warming way instead of in the negative ways I was more accustomed to.

It made me think, *maybe I really can help people?*

The most difficult aspect to reconcile was that all the things I was telling people to do when they felt depressed, hopeless or wanted to self-harm, were precisely the things I had *not* done myself.

People might well say, "Well you didn't do it, why should we?"

Well, here's the thing. I survived. I didn't die. As much as it wasn't a positive experience, and as awful as I felt about what I'd done for a long time afterwards, at least I could look back at aspects of that dark period and pick out positives that I could use to inform the future.

Some people aren't so lucky. Many people don't come out the other end of what I went through and can never look back with perspective and say, "I should have done this or that".

But I could, and I knew how powerful a position that put me in. I'd seen the other side for 30 seconds while I looked down at myself in my bedroom that night and I didn't want to go there.

It could have all been so different. I might not have been here to write this book. My family could easily have been left devastated, forever asking the question: "Why did she do it?" I'd have hated to leave them with that burden for the rest of their lives.

But here I am, one of the very lucky ones – so lucky that I even cut a useless tendon as it turned out. And to that extent I reckon it would be a crime to not offer my insights into what to do if you feel the way I felt.

It costs nothing for me to do that, and to keep talking about it all also helps my own healing process, which is still incomplete and might always be. I'm not perfect. You're not perfect. But I think the part that I never understood is that none of us are or probably ever will be. That's being human, and that's absolutely OK.

The other question people ask most often is, "Why didn't you just talk to someone?"

It's a valid question, and I must stress that it wasn't that I was abandoned during those dark two years. In fact there was no shortage of family and friends reaching out to me to offer help. I just didn't want it. I thought, given my competitive mindset as an elite athlete, that I could fix myself on my own. Indeed, I thought it would be weak to ask for anyone's help.

But I couldn't, I was in that emotional and irrational place. And by the time I realised that it was too late. I was way too deep, completely lost in a spiral of going on and off antidepressants and self harming. Everything in my life was closing in on me to the extent that I didn't know what to address first.

And then, when I realised how much of a mess my life was, I felt so much shame about it all and just thought I'd let everybody down, especially myself.

People might think, given how close we've always been, that my mother would have been the obvious person to talk to. But really, she was the absolute last person I was ever going to open up to.

My mother had done everything for me. She had believed in me when nobody else, including myself, had. She was the one that taught me to never give up. She was pushy, true, but she also knew that I had a gift for skating and that I wasn't old enough to understand that. She knew that if I didn't grab the chance I had when I was 15, I'd regret it for the rest of my life.

And she'd have been right. Despite how difficult it was coming to Nottingham when I was 15 and being thrown into the deepest of deep ends, I gradually found my own way, navigated all kinds of shit in the process, and became a multiple medal winner who travelled the world doing what she loves – a world champion and a world record holder. Imagine if I'd missed out on all of that?

So, having been given that opportunity, not to mention all kinds of financial and emotional support over the years, much of it from a distance, the last thing I wanted to do was make my mum feel that any of this mess was in any way her fault.

I didn't want anyone to feel that it was their fault. I had already had enough pressure on me without feeling guilty about what I'd offloaded onto them. I'd already put enough pressure on Shaolin to deal with me in the state I was in. He just couldn't handle it all, and so the last thing I wanted to do was to transfer that huge pressure onto somebody else I loved dearly. So, I just went it alone.

However, I'd strongly suggest that anyone else who finds themselves in a position that seems absolutely hopeless, to talk to someone about it first and foremost. Talk to *anyone* about it. What you're feeling in those moments where you want to cut yourself or jump off a bridge is pressure, the sense that everything is too much and that there are no solutions.

Talking to someone else, however, can only release some of that pressure while also allowing another viewpoint in, some added perspective, because in those moments when things seem most impossible for us, in my experience they feel that way because we've completely lost all perspective.

In my case, had I talked to someone, particularly someone who could be logical with me in a, "This isn't as impossible as you think it is and this is precisely why" way, it might just have helped me pull myself out of it.

The self-harm part of this is another element altogether, and similarly I find myself in a position where I'm offering people advice, while at the same time I'm not necessarily following it myself, despite the willingness being there.

One thing that is certain is that self-harm, in whatever form it comes, is not the answer to feelings of anxiety, depression or low self-esteem. In fact, self-harm, while it might initially feel good in the moment, always makes things worse.

On one hand, the physical impact just isn't pleasant. I've got ugly scars on my arms and wrist that'll be with me forever, a constant reminder for me (and anyone else in my life) of what I've been through. As someone who has always struggled with my self-image, the last thing I need is another part of my own body to be self-critical about.

And on the other, there's the mental side of self-harm – specifically the shame, disappointment and self-loathing that cutting only perpetuates. None of that is worth it. None of it works. There are other ways – and I say this in the contradictory position of being a person who has herself self-harmed reasonably recently in the absence of any other coping mechanism. I'd like to think it was a one-off, a weak moment, but because of how deeply I've conditioned myself to resort to it as my default, last resort coping mechanism, I can't ever be sure.

As 2019 rolled on and we went back into training again, I felt great. On one hand, I was finally injury free for the first time in a couple of years. On the other, having shared my story and come off antidepressants, I felt like a heavy weight had been lifted off my shoulders in the sense that, for the first time in perhaps forever, I could enjoy my skating for what it was, as opposed to being simply this essential counterbalance that admittedly I was pretty good at, but that was also required to keep my emotional self in check.

Unburdened, I was flying again. Whenever I got on the ice I felt like I did in those early days at the Centrum in Ayrshire. I can only describe it as pure, unadulterated joy – a feeling unlike anything else, and one that I'd spent a lifetime failing to replicate in other ways. Honestly, it felt as if the entire slate of my life had been wiped clean. Finally, at the age of 29, I was enjoying being me again.

However, if life has taught me anything, it's not to be complacent. As the saying goes, sometimes the light at the end of the tunnel is the light of an oncoming train.

In July 2019, I started feeling unwell, with abdominal pain that started off quite mild, then kept getting worse while also becoming focused on my lower-right side.

Honestly, I had no idea what it was. Abdominal muscles are vital for short track. They're what help you turn corners. I'd had niggles before; a pull here or a strain there. But this was different and constant.

I went to the doctor, who did a bit of an investigation, poked and prodded around the area doing what I was told was a standard test for appendicitis. And that was the diagnosis that came back.

I was admitted to hospital, assessed and it was discovered via a scan that not only did I have appendicitis, but that the appendix had actually ruptured.

Now, I'm far from the first to have a burst appendix but even I knew that it made a simple operation to remove an inflamed appendix into an emergency procedure to prevent much more serious abdominal conditions like peritonitis, which is caused when bacteria spills into the abdominal cavity and can, on rare occasions, be fatal.

I went into theatre and was put under general anaesthetic to get laparoscopic surgery to remove my burst appendix and to clean up the mess caused when it spilled bacteria everywhere.

Being a keyhole procedure that involves three small incisions, it's a much less invasive procedure than the open surgery that they used to have to do. Nevertheless, it's not pleasant, it is painful afterwards and in my case I had to go on a course of strong antibiotics to make sure there was no secondary infection. I was out of hospital in a day or two.

Having been injured for so much of 2018 and early 2019 and having only just got back into an uninterrupted training routine, the last thing I wanted to do was sit out any longer than I had to. With a full autumn season ahead, which was due to begin in November at a World Cup in Minsk, I didn't want to risk getting behind with my training routine when I was fit and injury free.

Within a week of the appendix surgery I was back in training. And as it turned out, that was far too early.

What I hadn't bargained for was how painful and tender my abdominal muscles were. I just couldn't turn corners. It was too painful.

The weeks and indeed months that followed were an exercise in absolute frustration. Determined not to let another season slip by, I pushed on regardless. But for every one step forward in aerobic fitness that I took, I also took two back from a niggling injury perspective.

For whatever reason I just kept picking up annoying, debilitating problems between returning from the appendix surgery and the end of the year: three different types of muscle tears, a couple of tendinopathies and then, finally, another random condition whereby my shin muscle had detached from the bone.

In the end, instead of going to the three World Cups in Bulgaria, Poland and Kazakhstan respectively, the only time I competed at all before Christmas during that 2019/2020 short track season was at an Invitational Cup meeting in Montreal in December, where I at least won a 1500m race.

After starting 2019 with so much hope, not much went right on the ice and, looking back, it all happened because I came back from the appendix surgery far too quickly and then consistently overtrained thereafter. My body just couldn't cope.

As if that wasn't enough, I then got a weird result in a doping test. Something was amiss.

When we looked into it a bit more, it transpired that it wasn't a problem from a doping perspective (that part of it was a mistake with the system) but there were still a couple of readings in the data that suggested I might have some kind of lingering kidney issue. As I sat in one of many doctor surgeries, I thought, *this is all I bloody need...*

When I first heard this problem and when I thought

about how I'd been feeling, I'd be lying if I said I'd been 100 per cent since the appendix surgery. As much as I'd tried and as hard as I'd pushed myself to try to reach peak fitness, I'd done so while feeling extraordinarily drained of energy all the time.

I suppose, given what I was told at the time of the surgery, that fact should have come as no surprise given that the suggestion was that it could potentially take four to six months to feel absolutely normal again. I just thought, being an athlete, I'd be able to get over it quicker. I was wrong.

Anyway, after a few back and forth trips to different doctors for a variety of tests which showed normal readings for haemoglobin and iron and loads of other things, we came to the conclusion that the marker we were seeing probably wasn't a kidney problem at all, but that it was much more likely to be a sign of my body still trying to recover fully in the aftermath of the surgery.

Regardless of what the causes were, when I assessed where I was in December 2019, I wasn't exactly happy. I'd come out of a disastrous year in 2018, got myself off medication and stopped self-harming. That was all positive.

On the downside, 2019 felt as if it had been a constant battle to stay fit and the impact of that meant that I had felt the odd wobble in my state of mind at various times.

On one hand, I started feeling those familiar creeping pangs of desperation and low self-worth because I hadn't been able to compete. Because of that, I had been tempted to self-harm again but had resisted and instead had opted for what I deemed to be the lesser of two evils, which was to go back onto antidepressants to keep my head straight instead of cutting myself to bits. On that front, once I'd gone back on the meds, I thought I had a grip on the situation.

On the other side of things, for all of the positive feedback I'd got for going public with my mental health struggles in April that year, social media had started getting me down to the point where I genuinely felt that it was contributing to my mental health problems rather than curing them.

I've thought about this a lot and if I'm really honest about it, I genuinely find the whole idea of social media to be such a complete head-fuck for me. A lot of athletes use social media to benefit and appease their sponsors and the like. But because I don't actually have any sponsors, when I post something on social media, I'm mostly doing it to make my life look good and to get affirmation back.

The reality of the situation is that, no matter how much I've grown as a person, conquered demons and become successful at what I do, there's still a part of me that dislikes myself and my body every bit as much as I did when I was back in Livingston at 14 years of age.

No matter what anyone says, or how clear it is to anybody else that I have the body of an elite athlete - the like of which would be the envy of many girls - I just don't see that.

All I think and all I see is that I'm fat – and given that I've reached the age of 30 and am probably at the peak of my physical wellbeing right now, it seems unlikely that I'll ever change this skewed image of myself that I carry around.

So, with that all being said, there is no doubt that getting positive comments from a picture of myself online makes me feel good, simply because it's the opposite of (a) what I was told at school and (b) what I feel about myself! And as vain and vacuous as it might sound, one of the main reasons I'm doing it is to make myself feel better. Let's be honest, that's why anyone does it, and anyone who says otherwise is lying!

I suppose you could say social media, and the reaction I get from engaging on it, is a bit like self-harm in that respect. But instead of cutting my wrist and getting a couple of hours of relief, I can post a picture of myself in my underwear with a nice filter and get the same if not more gratification from people who say, I look pretty or "a goddess" or, a bit more worryingly, "DM for collaboration" in the comments below. Sometimes, when things are getting me down, that little boost is all I need.

But, as much as the positive comments make me feel good, any negativity I get (I used to read all the comments but not so much now) makes me feel disproportionately worse, particularly if I'm not feeling great.

Strangely, it's not the directly abusive stuff that gets to me the most either.

If someone straight out says I'm ugly, or fat, or whatever, I'll probably just ignore it or even laugh it off. But if someone says something measured and targeted like, "You're not the role model to all these kids that you claim to be," (and someone did say that once) that would really get to me.

I'd think, *that's a bit unnecessary. You don't even know me.* And I have at times got drawn into getting into messaging privately with people, even though everyone tells me not to bother.

Occasionally you run into someone who's just on there to abuse anyone and everyone – and you do get plenty of those online these days.

But normally I've found that most people who say something unpleasant end up apologising in the end. And that's the conclusion of the dialogue.

Most recently I have realised that social media can actually be manipulated in your favour if you post the right things. If I want positive comments about how I look, I'll post filtered pictures of myself that people will clearly like. And sure enough, I will get positive energy back.

Equally, if I only ever posted endless pictures of me falling on my arse or getting disqualified in Olympic finals and crying, I'd inevitably attract a degree of negative attention in return.

The same obviously applies to mental health now as well. If I want to engage people and offer help and inspiration about mental health matters, I have learned to understand what kind of image and accompanying content to post. That's the positive side of social media. You can manipulate it to get the results that you want.

If there was anything that made me think about social media and, specifically, the role it can play in celebrity lives, it was Caroline Flack's suicide in February 2020. I wouldn't be understating things at all if I said that her death, and the circumstances that surrounded it, absolutely shook me to my core.

The reason for this was that, while she was obviously on an entirely different level of celebrity than I've ever been on, I nevertheless saw so much myself in her.

I knew from my own battles that mental health doesn't really care if you're a world champion, a celebrity or how many Instagram followers you have. If you're struggling, you're struggling – no matter who you are. Nobody, including a beautiful, talented TV presenter with seemingly everything in her life, is immune from the darkness and where it can push you.

More than anything, Caroline's death made me realise further how very fortunate I'd been on a couple of levels.

Firstly, as I've said so often, I'm one of the very lucky ones who survived a pivotal moment in my life where I'd felt I just couldn't go on living like I was.

Without knowing all the circumstances, she was less lucky.

Secondly, as much as I didn't physically talk to people in person while I was going through personal hell, at least I always had social media as a means of communicating on some level.

Again, I'm not sure what the specifics were at the time, but either she was unwilling or unable to express herself via that medium. I did read a post of hers a couple of months before her death, where she publicly said she had been advised *not* to use social media. And then when the statement she'd written that wasn't released until *after* her death referenced how one night could change a person's life forever, as someone who'd had one or maybe two occasions where I felt exactly that, I could feel the hairs on my neck stand on end as I read it.

I remember thinking, *imagine how different things might have been if she'd been able to post that.*

Maybe she'd have handled everything differently? Maybe she'd still be around today? Sadly, we'll never know. She wasn't one of the lucky ones.

Looking back, it would have been easy in the circumstances for my agent or UK Sport to have shut my social media down when I was clearly struggling, particularly if I'd started posting unhinged, nonsensical ranting that they thought might be damaging to my image in the long term.

Obviously my circumstances were different from Caroline's in that I wasn't being taken to court or anything like that. But they still gave me my freedom of expression because they knew how much I needed it.

I'll always be very grateful that the people around me allowed me to continue with my social media platform, no matter how dark things got in my personal life. Without it, I'm not sure where I'd have been.

So, as much of a double-edged sword as social media can be, I do believe that people who are struggling should be able to use it if they want to. If they can't talk to another human being about their problems face to face, like I couldn't, surely talking to the world via social media is preferable to not talking at all?

Equally, if someone feels that social media is toxic and is actually the reason why they feel so bad, they should be able to either disengage from it or shut it down altogether. One thing I have learned over all these years is that if something isn't doing you good, change it.

That's the way I see it at least. And while I've had my moments in the last couple of years: times where I've thought, *OK, I'm done with all this* or, less dramatically, *well, I'll just stop reading and responding to comments,* I've continued talking about my feelings on social media whenever I've felt like it and I don't think there's a downside to doing that.

Oddly, some of my friends and acquaintances do think there's a downside to me talking about mental health so much nowadays on social media – to the extent that I've actually lost friendships because of it. I'm sure a fair few people thought I was just whining and that I was making it all about me.

That, to me, is a bizarre take. I mean, I'd already lost a few friends while I was going through the worst of my problems. That I understand. I was an absolute lunatic. But to push me away now because I am actually trying to do something positive online for others *because* of my own past issues – that makes no sense to me whatsoever.

But that's just how it is. For whatever reason some people just aren't comfortable about the whole subject of suicide, mental health and the glaringly obvious connection between the two. I think it's a cultural issue unique to the UK.

Let's face it, until relatively recently, when someone committed suicide, it wasn't even reported as such. The report would just say something like, "so and so died suddenly at home".

And if it was reported as a suicide, rarely if ever was mental health referenced as the cause. It always felt as if both suicide and mental health came with such a stigma attached.

As crap as it is for the families of people who commit suicide for mental health reasons, awareness has improved a lot recently because of high profile instances like Caroline's. It's a shame that it needed something like that to bring suicide and mental health out into the open, but at least then the wider discussion it triggered can help other people who are struggling. That's the only glimmer of a silver lining in her terrible, tragic story.

For me personally, at this point in my life, having come this far myself in this quest to become a better person, that's why I keep talking about it: to perhaps help that one person who desperately needs to hear what I'm saying at a given moment.

When I look back at the position I was in during 2017, I can't help thinking how much of a difference it might have made to me if I'd heard an important message from the right person at the right time about mental health.

If I'd got the right message at the right moment and

understood that I had depression sooner, maybe I'd have got medicated sooner too.

Half the time I had no idea what was wrong with me. As awful as it sounds, I genuinely thought I was fucking mental, simply because I didn't know any better. Nobody else knew what was wrong with me either.

But….

If I had gone onto antidepressants sooner, maybe I wouldn't have been so manic and trained on through the pain in 2017. Maybe I would have stood up for myself when I felt I was being bullied on the run-up to PyeongChang.

Would I have gone to PyeongChang and won a medal if I'd understood my mental health sooner? Possibly. You just never know. But what I do know is that there's a chance that everything could have been very different for me if I'd been educated quicker.

So, no matter what anyone says, I won't stop trying to change perceptions about mental health in whatever way I can, simply because I know from the messages I've received already that my story has already helped people.

Knowing how much of an impact what I say can have, why the hell would I stop talking/writing about it?

Consequently, and this is the part of this where I have to decide what's really important to me at this point in my life, anyone I lose along the way because they're not comfortable with me in this role nowadays is quite frankly a sacrifice I'm perfectly willing to make.

I kid you not, saving someone who is struggling is more

important to me than the approval of someone who can't reconcile themselves, for their own screwed-up reasons, with this role I've created for myself as a mental health spokesperson. There are real lives at stake. It's my duty to do what I can, based on what I know.

The flipside for me, and there always is one when you look for positives as often as I do nowadays, is that my real friends, the ones who really do take the time to understand me, look out for me all the time now that I've gone public. And the reason they do is that they immediately recognise the signs when I retreat and go a little dark from time to time.

In such instances, I'll get a short, check-in message along the lines of – "Elise? Are you OK?"

If I'm OK, I'll say so. If not, I'll respond and say, "Not doing so great today, talk to you soon".

The way I see it, there's just no downside to that avenue of communication being open. Unlike those dark years, there at least *is* an avenue of communication. I can't even tell you how much of a difference that makes to know someone is there and communicating only promotes a level of healthy understanding on both sides. Anything that relieves the pressure in the moment can be vital in keeping you away from that place where you can't see an escape from your problems and your irrational brain takes over. When that happens, all bets are off.

Nobody knows that better than me.

Inevitably, in this new unofficial role, people often ask me what advice I'd give to someone who finds themselves in a situation like I was in: a razor blade at the wrist, standing on the edge of a cliff or with a handful of pills.

As I've said, I've never been a fan of vague motivational platitudes. As much as there may be a tiny grain truth in sayings like 'talking always helps' and 'it will get better', I always felt that if I simply churned that kind of stuff out whenever I was asked, I'd not only be being preachy (which I never want to be) but I'd also be going against everything that I've always believed in for motivation.

I need actual facts and actions that I can look at and see, clearly, how they are going to help. So with that in mind, I tried to formulate a few understandable guidelines with concrete actions that might be able to help other people.

When it comes to suicide and depression, I'd advise everyone, whomever you are, to check in on your loved ones regularly. As a self-harm survivor, I promise you that self-harm is not the way to heal – quite the reverse.

There are other ways to fight this. And the first thing I'd suggest is to go and talk to someone right away. They may not have all the answers, but the act of talking at all might just offer the kind of perspective or differing opinion that will make the difference and shift your mindset in a more healthy direction.

On the occasions where I don't feel like talking, instead of reverting to my old self-harm habits when I'm in a dark place, I just go to bed and sleep instead. Everything seems better when I wake up. Even if I have to take a sleeping tablet to get to sleep, that's preferable to cutting myself.

And if I don't feel like sleeping at that moment, I'll cook or clean.

On the other side, for the family and friends of a person who's going through a difficult time, I think it's important not to panic, because panicking will inevitably make your loved one feel that they have done something wrong.

Instead, a calm practical conversation is going to be much more productive. "OK, this is the situation, what are we going to do to fix this?"

That's the kind of thing I would have wanted to hear, and I suspect most others would too. Being practical removes the emotion from the situation, and when emotion is removed, someone is far less likely to be irrational in his or her thinking. In general, above and beyond anything, I think it's important to understand that mental health is inherently complicated. Overthinking it, in my opinion, only makes it more complicated.

Sometimes it's easier to simplify it and to just accept that you're going to have good days and bad days. These aren't a choice, and they don't make you a good person or a bad person depending on which way the pendulum has swung. Brain chemistry just is, and sometimes those fine chemical balances help you and sometimes they don't.

When you reach that point of acceptance, I think the problem becomes easier to manage because all of the guilt is removed. There is absolutely no shame in having struggles with mental health, anymore than there's shame attached to having asthma or suffering from a bit of athlete's foot.

Obviously, if it gets to the point where the fluctuation in your brain chemistry is impossible to manage via talking, good sleep, routine and nutrition, I'd personally suggest accepting some medication to balance things if offered it.

Like mental health itself, I think there's always been a weird stigma attached to antidepressant type medications, which doesn't really make sense to me. After all, if you've got a heart condition and there was a medication that you could take that would make your life better, you wouldn't hesitate to take it. The same should apply to medicines that are simply designed to address these subtle imbalances in your brain chemistry. If they can help, take them. And do so with no shame or fear of judgement.

Finally, and I accept this isn't always easy, I'd recommend not being around people who don't help you or make your situation worse. It might sound selfish, or even a bit ruthless, but if you were an asthma sufferer, you wouldn't just sit in a room that was full of dust and mould. You'd either move out of that room, or you'd get rid of the mould or dust.

Exactly the same applies to relationships. In the same way as getting rid of social media if it's making your problems worse is a good move, removing a person from your life who is doing the same is also the right thing.

As guilty as I've been about persevering with toxic relationships at times over the years, I'm at the point now where I've become self-aware enough to know that if something isn't working, I've got to change it. We're only here once. Life is far too short to do anything else.

TWELVE

STREET FIGHTER

AROUND THE TIME OF CAROLINE FLACK'S death, I'd got over the after-effects of the appendix surgery sufficiently to be back training, albeit I wasn't exactly in the best shape of my life.

By this point, having had a bit of an emotional wobble over the Christmas period, I decided to follow my own advice and go back on antidepressants again in order to balance my brain chemistry while I tried to focus on racing at the European Championships in Hungary and the two ISO World Cup meeting in Dresden and then Dordrecht the following week.

At the same time I changed coaches. For all the reasons I explained, it just wasn't working with Seung-jae, through no fault of his. I'm not sure what the circumstances of his departure were in the end either.

At that point I actually wanted Nick to come back. I even

asked the question at the time, but that idea was an absolute non-starter apparently. Instead, Richard Shoebridge, a former short track skater himself who competed with me in Sochi in 2014, took over. Although he had never specifically coached me in the past, he had been coaching other more junior members of the group for some time and was very well liked.

Immediately, things felt so much better. Shoey has many qualities, not least that he's a really enthusiastic and positive innovator when it comes to the programme generally, and he needs to be given our perilous funding position. But from my perspective, purely as a coach, he is much more aligned to the kind of way I think than Seung-jae was. He's another, like Nick, who is very fact-based and logical in his thinking.

In these early months of 2020, I wouldn't say I was particularly positive after a pretty ordinary showing at the Europeans where I went out in the heats of the 1000m and the semi-final of the 1500m.

The sad truth was that I was a victim of my own success. Let's face it – it doesn't get much better than being overall world champion. Sometimes it felt like I would always measure myself against a yardstick called 2017.

Consequently, I went to the World Cups despite not actually wanting to go. I didn't want to go because in real terms I'd only done seven weeks of training in total and had missed the previous five altogether before the Europeans. Again I thought, *I'm not ready…* Shoey thought otherwise.

"Elise, you are going, because competing is the best training you could possibly do right now," he said. "And it's not just the best physical training, mentally you need to get off your arse too."

During that first week in Dresden, I felt like my being there was the worst idea ever. After doing only four days of worthwhile training after the Europeans in Hungary, in the 1500m race I got dropped massively.

Immediately I thought, *I'm dead here.*

I was so tired. I just had nothing to give. I'd never felt as crap as I did in Dresden.

"I can't see how I'll ever get back to how I was in 2017," is the kind of thing I'd say to Shoey in moments of doubt that week. But again, he was always a step ahead of that kind of defeatist nonsense.

"Well, you say that," he'd say. "But you are doing this now, which is comparable with a time you did in a training session in February 2017. You're not actually that far away."

Shoey's consistently grounded approach was helpful and inspiring – and that kind of attitude helped me so much, and continually kept me out of that irrational place I can get into where, despite no real evidence whatsoever, I can talk myself out of pretty much anything.

Where my impression of my own ability at any given time is radically opposed to where that ability actually is. Honestly, it would take nothing for me to go home in the evening after what I thought was an indifferent training and think to myself, *I'm rubbish. Why am I even still doing this?*

The reality was that there really was cause for optimism at that second World Cup. I was slowly moving in the right direction and a large part of the reason for that was Shoey had taught me that not every training session had to be perfect.

He also instilled in me the idea that to constantly think that way was actually holding me back. "If you're always at your best, you'll never learn anything," he once told me. "Skating isn't just about winning," he also said.

That line was like one of those light-bulb moments you hear about so often. By going into training every day and thinking everyone was expecting me to be perfect for every second I was on the ice, I was actually doing my cause harm.

And I was so wrong. The reality was that nobody other than me was expecting, far less demanding, perfection – not even Shoey. All that was expected was for me to show up, skate, enjoy it and make progress into the bargain. Despite what I thought, I had nothing to prove to anyone, not even myself.

A week later, at the second World Cup meeting in Dordrecht, I felt completely different – like another person. I had energy. The old zest for the game was back. I skated much better and finished fifth in the 500m and was over the moon to do so. I wasn't exactly where I wanted to be, but I at least could see a return to my best form was possible.

Shoey had been right. As little training as I'd done, I'm a competitor at heart – a short track street fighter who needs to be fighting. So, I had to compete to find myself again, and fair play to him pushing me to do something that, to me, felt completely counterintuitive at the time.

When people ask questions like, "How do you define a good coach?" What Shoey did with me in early 2020 is a sign of a great coach. As much as I'm a headstrong athlete and I always think I know myself best; sometimes I just don't. Even the best athletes sometimes have to shut up, step back and trust.

Feeling distinctly freed by Shoey's coaching mojo, I was excited about the possibility of going to the Worlds unburdened, rolling the dice and seeing what happened. Soon however, all of this progress and positivity was put on hold when, with the World Championships in Seoul just a couple of weeks away, it started looking doubtful whether I'd even be there at all.

In the last race at the World Cup meeting in Dordrecht I got taken out, banged my head and was left with quite a nasty concussion.

From a place where I was thinking, *bring on the Worlds!* Now I was thinking, *this is absolutely shit. I doubt I'll even be able to go now.*

And then, before I had time to get any more pissed off and depressed about it, skating suddenly didn't matter anyway. The whole complexion of the world, what we knew and what was normal was changing in a way that nobody saw coming.

By mid March 2020, having been postponed at short notice, the World Championships in Seoul became a distant and insignificant memory as the Covid-19 pandemic hit and became pretty much the only subject anyone ever talked about. I was swept up in the hysteria, just like everyone else.

On a practical level for us, all the rinks closed and the off-season started early, as uncertainty about how the pandemic would play out across the world took hold. Like everyone, I don't think I had any sense as to how serious the bigger picture might get.

Just before Boris Johnson's mandatory stay-at-home message in late March, I was due to head up to Scotland to see my mum and to do some work on this book. This was a normal thing for me to do; my mum and I are still very close and I regularly go home or she comes down to visit me.

As I was driving north from Nottingham I started feeling increasingly ill to the point that, by the time I arrived in Livingston, I felt absolutely shocking. I had this dry cough, like I get when I've just finished a 500m race, and I was feeling hot and sweaty as well.

Obviously, these were pure Covid-19 symptoms based on what we knew at this early stage of things. I called my mum from the car. She was at home with my grandad at the time,

"I don't think I can come in," I told her. "I think I might have bloody Covid."

"Do whatever you think is best," was basically all that mum said.

As much all of us knew much less about the virus back

then, even in March 2020, I knew enough about how susceptible elderly people are to be able to make a decision about what I should do.

Consequently, feeling absolutely crap myself, I about-turned and drove straight back to Nottingham without stopping anywhere.

When I arrived in Nottingham I went straight to the hospital. I literally felt like I'd never felt before. I just couldn't breathe properly. By this point it was far worse than at the end of any race I'd ever skated in. I entered via the separate entrance the hospital already had in place to admit Covid-19 patients and got myself checked over.

My blood pressure was abnormally high, which is always a sign of something being amiss. But apart from that, they told me that my heart rate and blood oxygen levels were normal enough that I could just go home and rest. At no point did I get an actual Covid-19 test as this was obviously around the time where testing was relatively uncommon.

I went home and basically stayed in isolation for the next two weeks. If I lay down in bed or rested, I felt OK. But as soon as I stood up and tried to do anything, my breathing was so short and laboured that I just couldn't. I'd just start coughing uncontrollably. I've no doubt that I had Covid-19, and with hindsight I probably picked it up in the gym somewhere along the line because I'd been weight training during the previous two weeks given that the Worlds had been postponed.

Looking back on this weird time now, had I experienced

these symptoms a week or two earlier, I might not have thought anything of it. I would have probably just thought I was a bit tired or worn out at the end of the season and given it no more consideration.

I could easily have carried on and spread it to who knows how many other people. I probably would have stayed at my mum's and, given that she has lupus and my grandad is obviously elderly, things might have played out very differently. Thank god I turned back.

As it turned out, because she works in a hospital, my mum did indeed get Covid-19 and, because of her autoimmune condition, she ended up in hospital herself. Thankfully, unlike so many others, she was one of the lucky ones – as I was too. After a couple of weeks of feeling breathless and tired, I was back to full health again.

Despite being fit and healthy, by the time April came around when we'd normally be back on the ice and training, the whole country was stuck at home.

In the past, the idea of being at home 24/7, unable to train or race for an unspecified period of time, would have been my worst nightmare. I reckon I would have lost it and would have probably started self-harming within weeks if not days.

But for whatever reason, I just didn't feel like that during the national lockdown in 2020. If anything, the fact that we were all in the same boat motivated me even more. It felt like a reset I could really benefit from.

Instead of getting lazy and dropping out of routine, I

did the opposite. I was in bed early at night, up early the next day, eating well and planning my training routine even better than ever. I even managed to adapt my little garage into some kind of makeshift gym and I used the paved area up the side of it to do shuttle runs and dragging tires.

What was also great was that, in addition to persuading those holding the programme's purse strings to buy whatever equipment I needed to train from home, Shoey kept tabs on me right from the start to make sure that I was doing exactly as my schedule said I should be.

Without that kind of attention, I'm the kind of person that's inclined to go off at tangents. It's not that I think that, because I've been world champion, the programme doesn't apply to me. That's not it at all. It's more a case of whenever I'm left to my own devices my mind just wanders like a kid. I'll still be training hard and being disciplined about it, but I won't necessarily be doing what I'm meant to be doing at any given time!

Basically, I need a kick in the arse from time to time to keep me focused, particularly when I'm operating from home in the midst of a worldwide pandemic. Thankfully, Shoey recognised all of this and was never averse to keeping me in line. Every day I had to send over the readings from all my watt bike sessions and all the data from my Polar watch likewise went his way. Shoey was just strict enough with me, and instead of irritating me, his approach was a huge comfort and motivation.

As the weeks passed, I started viewing my sport, and

sport generally, differently. No, I couldn't lift heavy weights properly because I didn't have a proper rack at home and, yes, I did have dumbbells lined up on a picnic table in the garage in the most DIY of set-ups imaginable.

But regardless of all of that, I started not only realising how lucky I was to still be able to train at all in lockdown, but also how important just the basic routine of a sport can be for mental wellbeing. Because I'd have everything laid out in front of me since 2007, maybe I'd started taking what I had for granted.

Now I just think that sport of any kind is great for anyone's mental health.

Aside from the obvious physical benefits (and god knows the pandemic has shown us how much we all need to consider aerobic wellbeing going forward) there are so many ways in which it can have a positive impact because it forces a person to focus on something to which they can attach attainable goals.

To achieve those goals a person can build a daily routine that both fits into their lifestyle but also one that distracts them from other aspects of their life such as work, their state of mind, their relationships or any other area that might not be going so well.

The great thing about all of this is that while I am an elite athlete and one who has always used my sport to distract me from my mental health issues, the lockdown brought it home to me that you don't have to be an elite athlete to get that same benefit. You don't even have to be good at the sport at all; it's the fact that you're doing it on any level that's so important – as the many elderly people who make a point of getting up and going for a walk at the same time every day will attest to.

Occasionally, I've wondered how I might have coped with life if I hadn't been an athlete. Obviously it's partly a theoretical question because clearly I wouldn't have had to contend with the two disastrous Olympic experiences, but I still wonder how life might have gone. Sport and the discipline/distraction of training have been important to me since I was a young girl. It's hard to ignore those benefits.

So from a wider perspective going forward, when this pandemic is over, if there's anything that the authorities and sporting bodies need to focus on, it's how to encourage everyone, regardless of their age, sex, colour sexual orientation or financial means, to participate in some kind of sporting activity that creates a degree of manageable discipline in their life. As much as the activity itself is beneficial, I always tell people who ask me about how to combat mental health struggles exactly the same thing: **stay in a routine!**

I took my own advice and stuck to my routine throughout the early summer months of 2020 and I managed it with only the weekly check-in Zoom calls to remind me that I was even still part of an elite team of athletes.

The funny thing about all of this is that, on two fronts, physical and mental, I was fitter than I'd been in a long time during lockdown.

While I obviously couldn't get on the ice, because I was

forced to be more resourceful and to train more organically doing routines that I might not have otherwise, from a full body perspective I was probably in better fitness shape than I might have been if the pandemic hadn't happened.

Mentally I was in a similarly fresh place too, living with my boyfriend Leigh for the first few months or so and keeping it all nicely balanced with that daily routine I prized so highly.

Given that it was looking highly unlikely that we'd get back on the ice at all until September or October at the earliest, my concern as the summer months dragged on was whether they'd even be able to reopen the National Ice Centre again from a financial perspective.

Even in good years, I'm told it's a marginal proposition from a profitability standpoint. I'd heard that in 2019, even with all the concerts they put on in the off-ice season, they still came out of it all £750,000 in debt. The only hope in the midst of the pandemic was that, because it was the National Ice Centre and home to the best athletes in the country, maybe it would be eligible for some kind of Covid-19 relief grant.

The other possibility, I suppose, was that the whole skating programme could have been moved to Sheffield permanently, which wouldn't have been a big deal given its proximity to Nottingham. For a while it was all up in the air.

Again to Shoey's credit, he tried everything he could to keep the remote programme varied and positive while all this uncertainty hung over when ice rinks would reopen, if they ever did at all.

The biggest issue was, as much as I was able to find a positive in the lockdown situation by using the time to make fitness gains, obviously the lack of physical skating meant that we just couldn't keep technique sharp. If you don't skate, your muscles detrain and become unaccustomed to the movements required to be dynamic and stable at the highest level.

As an alternative, Shoey suggested we all do inline skating at home. He was really enthusiastic about it and I guess, as the head of the programme, he had to be because really that was the only option there was.

In theory, it was a good idea and was absolutely better than nothing in that you could at least learn some new aspects of stability. But we soon realised that inline was weather dependent in the sense that it's just not safe to do it in the rain. That ruled out a good few days, as I recall.

The other problem with inline is that it's really nothing like short track from a technique approach. From the outside it probably looks similar, but believe me it isn't. Where all of short track's power comes through the heels, inline is much more akin to figure skating, where all the push comes through the toes.

Inevitably, after a few months of enthusiasm and accepting the position we were all in, I got to the point where, as much as I could attain a degree of fitness and hold things at a certain level, I couldn't really make any significant gains without the day-to-day attention of the coaching staff.

As much as you can do Zoom calls like the rest of the world was doing throughout lockdown, it's just not the same when you're trying to coach a team of elite athletes – any more than it's the same when you're trying to maintain a relationship with a family you're used to seeing in person on a daily basis. There comes a point where you just can't make any more progress. When you're just grasping onto anything you can, you reach a plateau where there's nothing left to grasp and things just get stale instead.

Just when things were indeed getting a bit strained in late June and early July, a bombshell hit the short track world when the Dutch skater Lara van Ruijven passed away at the age of just 28.

Lara was one of the girls in the short track world that I was closest to. I had spoken to her around the beginning of the lockdown, just as I was starting to go back into training in my garage. She knew that I'd struggled at various times over recent years so she was really just sending me some positivity as if to say, "I see you. And I'm here for you". That was the last time I ever spoke to her.

Oddly, I'd messaged her a couple of days before we all heard that she was in intensive care and I didn't hear back. At the time I thought, *oh, she hasn't replied. That's a bit weird.* But obviously, while I didn't know it at the time, she was already in a coma at that point.

I never really heard all the details of what happened to Lara. I don't think anyone really divulged them either. All

I know is that she passed out at training and was only ever conscious for 24 hours thereafter.

My understanding of it was that she had a bleed on the brain caused by some kind of autoimmune disorder. I also knew that she'd had surgery on her shoulder earlier in the year and there were suggestions that there had also been complications as a result of that. Once they'd operated on her twice to stop the brain bleed, apparently the family only got two hours' notice before she passed away. It all happened so fast.

The whole episode not only upset me hugely, but the whole short track world was devastated by Lara's death. There's never an easy time for a young person to pass away, but for it to happen in the midst of a pandemic when there was already so much heartache around, that only made things harder.

What I do know for sure is that I'll really miss Lara. I know everyone says the same thing about people who die but she literally was the nicest girl in short track. She was kind, bubbly, and always there for her friends. Lara was by far the most humble world champion I've ever known and I still can't process that she's gone.

As the summer moved towards autumn, I won't deny that I started getting a bit pissed off by the government's priorities as I saw them.

Firstly, let me just say that I never had a problem with the national lockdown where, for everyone's benefit, the government didn't want anyone doing anything. That was all fair enough – and we weren't technically due back on the ice until May or June anyway as it was, so it wasn't as if we missed out on much at the initial stage of the lockdown.

But when things started opening up again in August, we, elite athletes doing something that promotes fitness, good mental health and positive values, couldn't get back on the ice in Nottingham for love nor bloody money. Meanwhile, the government obviously thought it was more important to let people go to pubs.

I just couldn't get my head around that decision at the time, and I had no problem with getting on social media and having a right good rant about it. There we all were in the midst of a pandemic, where those with unhealthy lifestyles were clearly more at risk of dying of the virus than fit people, yet, at the same time, the government prioritised a less healthy leisure activity like drinking alcohol (or eating out for that matter) over sport.

I think they got that so wrong. And while I sat at home watching people getting excited about being able to get a pint for the first time in months, I was bloody raging about not being able to get on an ice rink for my job.

And that wasn't all.

My other gripe was that athletes who appeared to be seen as having a higher status than short track speed skaters had no problem accessing facilities and in many cases their sports continued, albeit with no crowds.

Everyone seemed willing and able to bend over backwards to create this whole 'bubble' infrastructure to make it all work for them – all at vast cost to someone.

Meanwhile, I, a triple world champion, was doing weights in my garage knowing that I'd still be expected to get medals when I next competed. What a joke!

Let me be clear and say that in no way did I blame UK Sport or the EIS – the English Institute of Sport – for any of these problems. In reality, neither of those bodies had any control over what was happening nationally.

To me personally, they were both my lockdown saviours. Whenever the issue of buying the equipment I needed to train at home came up, they always helped me where they possibly could and I was and am extremely grateful for that support. I certainly couldn't have funded gym equipment on my own. I had to get an old watt bike of my mother's shipped down from Scotland. As it turned out, it was September until we eventually got back on the ice, initially in Sheffield and thereafter at Nottingham.

On the first few days back, because we'd all been skating on in-lines as per Shoey's suggestion, none of us could turn the corners because we were all so used to pushing through our toes. For a day or two we all looked like beginners but gradually it all came back after time on the ice.

Having already been pushed forward to a speculative date in October from the original date in March, the 2020 World Championships were officially cancelled, leaving us with the likelihood of no competitive skating whatsoever in 2020.

Having done so well for so many months and having

felt positive about everything in my life, I started feeling those familiar feelings of extreme anxiety building in the background at the turn of the year.

I'd gone through an unpleasant break-up with my boyfriend, Leigh, who I'd dated, split up with and then taken back, all within the space of around 18 months.

During the lockdown of 2020, I can't deny that having someone around for company helped my general state of mind. Nobody particularly wants to be alone when the whole world is going through a pandemic. Also, while he was living with me, Leigh was also contributing to household expenses, which was obviously helpful too at a difficult time.

The problem was that, over time, it became obvious that we were not the right person for each other.

I guess I'd partially known that all along, but had turned a blind eye to it all amid all the turmoil of the Covid-19 pandemic.

After it had ended and as he packed his stuff, I thought, *I've only got one more Olympics. I can find a man anytime.*

Not long afterwards, the European Championships were cancelled leaving only the World Championships in Dordrecht, still tentatively scheduled for early March 2021.

With all the stress of the break-up from Leigh, I was already wound up enough without worrying about the Worlds and whether they'd happen at all given that the UK was in the midst of a second Covid-19 wave.

At the same time I was also getting into a few petty

arguments with my teammates, which just isn't like me at all.

Then, to top it all, just when I needed to stay fit and healthy, one of the lads skated through me at training and I picked up another terrible concussion. This was a really bad one. I've never hit my head so hard in my life.

All of a sudden, after a long period of positivity, I started to wobble mentally when faced with the possibility that, through no fault of my own, I could find myself missing the World Championships after basically only skating once competitively in a period of almost two years.

I was so frustrated, having had so many injuries in 2019, to get myself fit only to have a freak head injury threaten all of my plans again.

I'm not ashamed to admit that I self-harmed again during this time. I didn't go back into it as deeply as I had done in the past; I'd call it just a momentary relapse. But I still did it, and to that extent I think it's important to say so.

I feel that way because I remember hearing Dame Kelly Holmes admit that she'd self-harmed at certain points of her career when she was injured and unable to train.

At the time, I was as shocked as anyone to hear that because she'd never given any indication it was going on at the time. She never mentioned the pain she felt. Instead, she kept it inside until her career had ended and that made me sad.

So, the most important thing to know about me sharing my mental health journey is that how I present it publicly will always be real and never in any way sanitised. I don't want to keep these emotions inside. To do so makes things so much worse. So, if I'm doing well, you'll know about it and I'll explain what's happening in my life that's making me feel that way. Equally, if I'm feeling shit and am spiralling down a familiar path, I'll relay that too, simply because if I didn't do that, my story wouldn't be in any way relatable to the thousands out there who are riding a similar rollercoaster every day in life.

The point is therefore that this *is* a rollercoaster. Yes, I want to be there to offer comfort to people and, yes, I want to use this relatively small platform I have to talk about the subject of mental health. But the truth is that I'm still dealing with my own problems every day, and that, the way I see it, is an integral part of the message.

I'm not someone who is sitting on high, an untouchable semi-celebrity tossing down the occasional word of wisdom or nuggets of vague advice. I'm not just saying, "It'll get better" or "choose happy", while sitting under a tropical fountain, cross-legged in some sort of yoga pose while hummingbirds circle my head like a halo.

Instead, I'm there, in the bloody trenches in my half-finished extension in Nottingham, living this mental health struggle daily and alongside every single one of the people who follow me and find some kind of comfort from whatever I post on Instagram.

To that end, I owe it to every one of those people to not hide when things go wrong, when I, without any logic whatsoever, decide to come off my meds in the midst of a relapse and start cutting myself again.

These are the realities of my mental health struggle, and it's a constantly evolving battle that I'm going to document regardless of how disappointing/confusing it might be for some people to hear that I still, under certain circumstances, revert to cutting myself with a razor blade.

The whole ditching my meds thing is a weird one – even I have to admit that. I mean, you'd think, when things are at their worst, I'd want all the help from medication I can bloody get!

But in that moment, I don't think that's what I think. In fact, I don't think I'm thinking at all. I just panic, abruptly stop taking them, and then everything just gets worse for a while and I retreat into that familiar place where the only thing I can handle in my life is training.

I don't answer calls and I don't reply to messages. I remove read receipts from my message apps, even though I know everyone will know that I've read them anyway. I don't want to communicate with anyone; I don't want to think about anything or deal with any problems, complex or trivial. All I want to do is train and then sleep. And that's what I did in March 2021 as the demons congregated in my head.

But like always, I emerged.

If that night in December 2018 taught me anything it was that, no matter what, I would always emerge from the darkness. It was such an important realisation that came with a positive and a negative.

The positive was that I realised that, having been through everything I'd been through and survived it all, life really doesn't hold many fears at all going forward.

Yes, I might fall in a race and, yes, I might owe the bank a few grand on my overdraft. But regardless, the sun really will always rise in the morning. I know these things are surmountable if I always focus on the future and moving forward with fixed goals in mind.

The negative, if you could call it that, was that it made me realise that mental health issues aren't just a one-off for me. Because my brain chemistry is uniquely mine, the feelings that those chemicals trigger are also mine. Therefore I have to live with them indefinitely, just as I would if I had a skin condition that flared up every once in a while under certain conditions.

As weak as I felt for going back on my tablets when my head cleared, I also knew that they were necessary and nothing to be ashamed of.

THIRTEEN

DOUGH

I CAN'T SAY THAT IT WAS A GREAT SURPRISE to me when I copped some snarky abuse in the papers in March for getting a job working in my local Pizza Hut. "World champion speed skater Elise Christie working as Pizza Hut delivery driver to make cash for Winter Olympics," *The Sun* said.

They probably thought they'd caught me doing something, in classic tabloid 'gotcha' style, but really it only confirmed to me what I've always felt about the shit attitude that's prevalent in this country about financial struggles and the concept of debt more generally: that it's weak and something to be ashamed of. *The Sun*'s headline, for all they probably hoped it would embarrass me, merely confirmed that awful stereotype.

The truth of the matter – and this should be blatantly obvious by now – is that short track speed skating isn't like a football career at the top level, where someone earns a fortune while they're playing and then, in theory, retires to live comfortably off what they made for the rest of their lives.

The sad fact is that life is something that needs navigating *in spite* of a career in short track speed skating, even at the elite level at which I've been operating.

As I said previously, I willingly went into it knowing this, and that not only would I not make a fortune, but also that I'd probably be in significant debt at the end of it all.

And, guess what? That is the case! But the fact of the matter is, erratic spending spree when I was losing my mind aside, I would still have been in debt at the end of my career, no matter what I'd done. I had no alternative.

Short of getting a parallel job and accepting that my skating would have suffered as a result, what other means of earning money were there? We don't get sponsors like the summer games athletes do. Even that's a bit nuts when you think about it.

Not to put anyone down, but there are athletes in athletics who are sponsored by Nike just because they once competed at a European Championships. Meanwhile, here I am, a *10-time* European Champion, sponsored by absolutely nobody. It feels like there's just no balance, and instead of making me feel in any way bitter, it makes me feel sad for our sport and its long-term future.

The biggest laugh of all is that people still love to say, "Oh yeah but she's funded!" like that materially changes anything. Yes I'm funded, but funding really only covers the absolute basics of what's needed to compete in the sport: paying a mortgage, bills, skates (£700 a pair by the way) – it all adds up and there's certainly nothing left at the end of the month for much else. I certainly don't go on regular flash holidays or have second homes, and I'm fine with all of that.

But at times it really is a bloody struggle to stay afloat, and I've never understood why British culture vilifies poverty, debt and general financial difficulties like it does. I remember when the Olympic badminton player Gail Emms got stick for selling stuff on eBay. What else was she supposed to do? More athletes are struggling than we know.

Surely being resilient through adversity by doing whatever you can to stay afloat in difficult times is a much more admirable human quality than falling into a life of inherited wealth and entitlement anyway? Yet, it's the latter group who are lauded so much at everyone else's expense while those struggling are viewed as some kind of subclass to be looked down upon.

I'm in an even more awkward position whereby the average man or woman doesn't really have any understanding of the financial realities of my sport. They see me on TV at the Olympics in the red, white and blue, look at my social media, see me being interviewed in newspaper articles in *The Times* or wherever and just say, "She must be loaded!"

Given the way that some athletes are treated in the media I don't blame anyone for having that view. I probably would too if I wasn't an athlete. Even the staff at the Pizza Hut in Nottingham thought the same when I started working there. The first night I walked in, everybody stopped what he or she was doing and just stared as I walked from the door to the counter.

"What, the hell, are, you, doing here?" someone said.

"I'm here to get paid, just like the rest of you!" I told them.

"Oh come on. We thought you'd be well minted?" they said.

"Yeah, yeah, sure. I wish…" I just said.

And from there, the ice was broken. That was all that was ever said about me working in a regular job. Because I went in there with absolutely no airs and graces, everyone accepted me as just another employee.

As much as I do get a few modest privileges, mainly in terms of having shifts scheduled to help me while I'm training, I'm basically just treated like any other member of staff and that's exactly what I want.

On a number of levels, I'm absolutely fine with the Pizza Hut job and I certainly don't have any shame whatsoever in pulling on the staff uniform and heading in there for a shift. If I did, you wouldn't see me posting stuff like, "Lessssss go…from daytime athlete to evening pizza maker ;)" on my Instagram for the whole world to see.

As much as the money really helps me, especially after splitting up with a boyfriend who was contributing to bills (plus I'm on 'B Card' funding currently), I genuinely like the camaraderie of being in a group of great people with whom I've got something in common that's got absolutely nothing to do with skating.

Don't get me wrong, I love the skating programme and it's been my life. But I realise that I do like finding things outside of the short track bubble. And I'm already at the point – a couple of months into this job – where I think that having something else to do will actually help my skating in this final push towards Beijing. I'll probably keep working at Pizza Hut when I come back from the Olympics as well.

What people, including me, often forget is that since the age of 15 I've never known anything else apart from the athlete life. I guess when you're in that reality, and when it's been as chaotic as mine has, you lose track of that fact sometimes. I guess I assume that everyone has lived the kind of life I have, when actually very few women of my age have.

This is brought home to me especially when I'm around old friends and they start talking among each other about things they did when they were growing up.

As they're talking, I'm often thinking, *well, I didn't do any of that…*

Occasionally, even though I have squeezed in isolated bits and pieces of education throughout my career, I have found myself thinking about the education that I didn't get over the years: university, college or something more vocational that might train me for a career after skating.

You do come across athletes that do manage to pursue their career and study, but usually they're either in a sport that takes up less time than short track, or they don't make it to the very top of their sport. There always appears to be a trade-off. It's very rare that someone is able to study for a degree and be a world champion.

I chose to give everything I had to my sport. I made a decision to not pursue any education in the build-up to Sochi. It went the way it did. Then, I made the same decision going into PyeongChang, and it went a similar way. I'm fine with all of that. That's what the eight-year plan dictated and I wouldn't change anything about that even if I could turn back the clock.

Inevitably, however, there's a part of me that occasionally sits there and thinks, *could I have done more with my life?*

Similarly, I do think back from time to time and feel that I missed so much of the social aspect of being a teenager, particularly when it came to boyfriends and relationships and so on. The truth is, boys didn't really understand the lifestyle I was leading when I was 17 or 18 – the training, the discipline, the mindset and the travelling.

Inevitably, I lost a lot of boys because of that, not to mention a lot of regular friends – all of whom just could not relate to my life. I don't blame any of them for that, either. After all, as much as I get on great with my own brother Jamie, he has never understood my life anymore than I've understood his. And that's absolutely fine!

The million-dollar question I occasionally ask myself

is, "If I could go back, would I have made the decision to become an athlete?"

The honest answer is that I just don't know.

Obviously, given what I know now and what I've achieved, I wouldn't give anything back. But, given the decision over again, if I'd known my career was going to go like this, I'm just not sure what I'd say.

Obviously, not having done other sports (although I did have a very brief thought about switching to cycling after Sochi when I did a programme for Sky Sports and I found out I was good at it), I don't know if all sports people feel like this and I've never asked them. But one thing is for sure: short track is a hard, hard sport to be in for a career, especially in this country.

You've got to *really* want to do it, and while you do so, you also have to come to terms with the fact that the gains other than winning medals might be negligible. Equally, you can medal all year long, but the one race in which you don't can be career defining. I know this better than most. It's truly a mad sport from that standpoint, and in a twisted, masochistic kind of way, that's part of the attraction.

So, when mum sometimes asks, "If you'd known what it would be like, would you have chosen sport as a career at all?" I guess my answer is, "Yes I'd have chosen sport. Just maybe not *this* sport!"

But for now, that's all pointless speculation. I'm here, with my last Olympics 10 months away. Deeper reflection will no doubt come later. But the Pizza Hut job will continue to be part of the plan for as long as I can make it all fit in my life.

From a broader perspective, people forget that, one way or another, I have to give at least some thought to what I might do with my life after Beijing. I'll be 31, and while I'm not suggesting that a career with Pizza Hut is in my long-term plans, I think it's sensible for me to have something formal to put on my CV for when I do go out there into the world – maybe into a career as a paramedic, or maybe if I decide to join the police.

I've considered both of these jobs. I'd like something where I have to be part of a responsive team, ready and willing to help people. That's the kind of work that would appeal to me.

I'd still need some kind of adrenaline fix. It would be nice for once to have a regular, reliable income too – and not one that depended on me hitting stressful athletic targets to secure funding going forward.

As I've said, I'll end this athlete career in debt and while that's not ideal, I've reached a point where I only look forward, believing that in six or seven years I'll look back on the situation I'm in now financially and think, *I'm glad I made it out of that.* Even to feel like that is such huge progress for me. Not so long ago, all I would have thought is, *there is no way out of this.*

*****

We are back on the ice in Nottingham training all out for Beijing. The World Championships in Dordrecht in the Netherlands happened, but we weren't allowed to be there because the Dutch government placed travel restrictions on athletes travelling from the UK on account of our sky-high Covid-19 case rate at the time.

It was all so disappointing and I actually felt like I'd have been going there in pretty good skating shape.

As it turned out, the Worlds were a bit of a weird one anyway, with the pandemic continuing to affect not only travel, but also people's states of mind. And it's not over yet.

Canada has been on and off the ice because of Covid-19. Even still, one of my main rivals, Kim Boutin, chose not to go to the Worlds at all because she hadn't been feeling mentally great about everything that's going on in the world.

Elsewhere, China has had ice the whole time but weren't there; Korea doesn't even have a national team at present and have been skating in clubs instead. They weren't there. The Japanese have had various training issues and weren't at the Worlds. Italy has been on and off the ice with Covid-19, as have Hungary, who has had Covid-19 in their team on two occasions.

The only team that's had a mostly uninterrupted time of things is the Dutch. They've had ice throughout the pandemic and are consequently skating faster than anyone else right now.

But then they also lost Lara in the midst of all of this tumultuous year. It hasn't exactly been easy for them either.

The upshot of all of the above is that, as we stand, in August 2021, with the Olympics in Beijing just a few months away in January 2022, I have absolutely no idea where everyone is in terms of who'll be turning up in China best prepared. All bets are off in that respect. It is truly the most bizarre lead-in to an Olympic Games ever.

Incidentally, in spite of what some people are predicting regarding either a Covid-19 related problem or a boycott of some kind, I think the Olympics will go ahead in Beijing, with or without crowds. I don't have any concerns around that at all. Knowing what I do about China, I'm pretty certain that they will do anything they can to run an Olympic Games successfully while the rest of the world can't function. And they don't need the income from the crowds anyway; they can do it all without audiences.

It has been the most bizarre of build-ups and it's certainly going to be interesting to see what happens. From my personal perspective, while I'm not in the kind of shape I was in during 2017, I'm skating well and am a lot closer to it than I've been in the last two or three years.

My goal in the months leading up to Beijing isn't just to get back to my 2017 ability; I want to surpass it. And with that in mind I believe that a medal in the 500m in Beijing is achievable, especially given that I have heard that they'll be running the distances in a different order from usual. That'll be to my advantage, I strongly believe. The 1500m won't get in the way.

Inevitably, it is impossible to look at Beijing, and the

Olympics in general, without the occasional, *what happens if I fail again?* type of thought going through my mind. Given the drastic nature of how my last two Olympics have gone, I wouldn't be human if I didn't have those thoughts.

But there's a difference this time, and maybe, just maybe this will be the key.

Because of everything I've been through, I know what rock bottom feels like and I've eyeballed it and come back. From that perspective, what can possibly happen in Beijing that would be any worse than what's gone before?

Granted, I've yet to be disqualified for a double false start, so there is that I suppose! But seriously, no matter what happens in Beijing, I know that it's my last chance for an Olympic medal, so rather than go out there fearful of failure, I have decided that I'll go there carrying the kind of youthful joy and daring that propelled me to this place where I'm about to go to my fourth Olympic Games. Of the many things Shoey has taught me over the last few months, it's that I've got to enjoy skating for skating's sake.

Seriously, what have I got to lose? If I didn't deep down in my gut feel that it's my destiny to win an Olympic medal, I've had plenty of opportunities in my career to walk away and say, *OK, Elise, just stop. It just wasn't meant to be.*

But, while I'd love an Olympic medal because it's the one thing in my skating career that I don't have, I also know that winning one or not will not define me as a human being.

I know my career has been great by any standards; I've done more for British short track than anyone in the history of the sport. No matter what happens in Beijing, nobody can take that away from me.

But beyond that, the experience of being an athlete has taught me so much about myself that I'm as excited about the next stage of my life as I was when I was embarking on the first phase when I was 15. I still want to have a normal life; I'd still love to get married and to have kids.

But for now, Beijing is the only thing I'm going to focus on. While my social media will continue, especially focused on the mental health side of things, I will step away for a few months to give all this one last shot. The last thing I need is to get trolled day and night at my last Olympics. In any case, Instagram and Twitter will still be there when Beijing is all over, and believe me you'll be hearing about it on there if I do win a medal.

In general, as much as I've accepted that I will always have the occasional relapse, the aspect of my life that I take most encouragement from is my self-awareness – and this is an attribute that I think I've always had since I was a kid, but until relatively recently didn't understand fully.

I actually believe that at the very core of things, I am an outgoing, goofy person who doesn't take too many things very seriously. All my friends nowadays see me as that, and, in interviews, that's the image I like to put across, along with the suggestion that I'm just a bit of a blonde airhead who isn't very intelligent.

I, however, know different. Maybe I'm smarter than many people think? But that's not for me to say...

So I've always known all of this about myself. I know fundamentally what kind of person I am. But with hindsight I believe that my childhood issues not only made me take on a new persona as this shy, weak, anxious girl at a young age, but also that, because of the relentless nature of a career that began when I was still basically a child, I was never able to escape that persona, as much as I knew inside that it was a false one.

Then, when all the misfortune piled upon me over the years: rape, death threats, bullying etc. I had even less opportunity to shake off the anxious feelings because I was so deep in the emotional turmoil that all these traumatic events combined to inflict upon me year after year.

But now I'm different.

I drew a line in the sand in December 2018. I know what my faults are and I own them every day. I might not always have the solutions and it might take me a while to address things when I do, but at least I have the basic self-awareness to be able to say, *Elise, this is wrong, something has to change.* To be able to acknowledge that at all is half the battle. From there, the only way is up for me.

Interestingly, I'm able to see my dad through slightly different eyes because of the way my own life has gone.

When I was young, all I knew was that he wasn't physically there and that life was tougher for my mum because he wasn't.

At no point did I consider *why* things were as they were with him. It's taken me 30 years to understand myself, far less anyone else. Over the years, my mum and I have remained extremely close. Even nowadays, from a distance of 500 miles, she likes to take an active role in my life to the extent that sometimes it's a bit annoying. Even today, she still rings me a couple of times a day! But deep down I know that she's only doing it because she cares about me so much and that she has skated, in a figurative sense, every step with me along the way.

The relationship with my dad I'd describe as just about OK. In normal Covid-free times he'll come down to Nottingham and stay in the area. We get along just fine on a surface level. But I'm sure we both know that there's something missing that can never be replaced: that he wasn't present while I navigated this completely abnormal life I've lived.

However, because of how my early life informed the entirety of mine thereafter, I've been able to look at his experiences and understand more about why he is like he is. He came from a difficult upbringing; his own dad drank and was abusive. That life affected my dad deeply, and in a twisted kind of way I'm grateful that he did leave my mum when we were so young because, while we had to endure his absence, Jamie and I were never beaten or abused. That's a positive. There's *always* a positive.

So on some levels I understand my dad more and am able to forgive his shortcomings somewhat, simply because I know how much life can change a person. But what I struggle to deal with – and this is where he and I will always differ – is that, as shit as his life has been, he has never really done himself any favours. Even today, knowing all the damage it has done, he still drinks, while I just roll my eyes. At no point has he ever stopped and thought, *maybe this isn't working? Something has got to change.*

While I'm semi-empathetic to him, Jamie isn't. Whether it's because he's on the spectrum and doesn't process emotions in the same way as a normal person might or whether he just doesn't want a relationship with his dad because he, unlike me, remembers the night he left, I don't really know. Either way, what is clear is that Jamie has decided he's done with him. There is no relationship. It's a shame for both sides, but I totally respect that's his choice.

Nowadays, as close as we were when we were kids, Jamie and I aren't exactly the kind of brother and sister who are inseparable. While I developed my athletic career, he continued down the academic path he embarked on as a kid. He still lives close to where we grew up and he's still really into mathematics, science and university, to the extent he often says things like, "I have absolutely no idea why you are doing what you're doing!"

But now I think I understand more than ever what I'm doing and why. In this last season before I go off and do whatever else, I don't think I've ever understood myself better than I do now. Although I don't see it myself, people tell me I've grown so much as a person in the last couple of years. And, I suppose, when I watch the documentary I did for the BBC in 2018 in the lead-up to PyeongChang and then the clip I did with Sky Sports in 2020, then yes, I suppose I do see where I've changed.

In 2018, I was a girl in turmoil who couldn't stand up for herself, and now I'm a 30-year-old woman who has been through a lot and who clearly understands herself better and why she does what she does.

Whatever happens going forward, I'll be fine. And that includes the Olympics in 2022.

Looking back, for most of my career I reckon I thought only like a speed skater in the sense that I only wanted to be the best speed skater in the world. So, as disappointing and harrowing as those two Olympic disasters were for all kinds of different reasons, for me, it really didn't matter if I won an Olympic gold or a World Championship gold, because either meant that I was the best speed skater in the world at that time.

But now I see it a little differently, and that's only because I've become a lot worldlier in my outlook. Once I won an overall World Championship, it became less important to me, but only because I'd done it.

While for the insiders within our sport, an overall World Championship is indeed a greater accolade than an Olympic gold in a single distance, for the man or woman on the street, the world at large who know little about the sport, an Olympic gold carries a different type of indisputable cache (not to mention the commercial opportunities that come with it). So from that perspective it isn't just about what I feel about me; it's also about the world's perception of me.

To that end, of course I'd like to be referred to as Elise Christie, an Olympic champion, but not so much for those commercial opportunities. Skating for me has never been about that.

Money and opportunity isn't why I speed skate. If it were I'd have retired long ago in disgust. For me it's much more because it's something that remains undone in my career. In my life, an Olympic medal is missing. But whatever happens, I repeat, the Olympics won't define me.

This I understand now, and for that reason I know that I'll be going to Beijing with a slightly different type of motivation driving me.

Personally, I know I'm one of the best woman speed skaters in the world. That's indisputable. But I want to prove that I can take that next step and be accepted on a broader level as an Olympic champion. I think I can, or I wouldn't be putting myself through all this shit again!

Inevitably, given everything that's happened to me, journalists often ask me questions like, "So what will you do if it all goes wrong for you in Beijing, just like the last two Olympics?"

When they ask me that, I think they think they know the answer already – and that it'll be something along the lines of, "I'll be fine. I'm older now. It won't affect me the same".

That isn't the answer they get. Because I understand myself so well now, I know that I'll absolutely fall apart if Beijing goes tits up for some reason. I fully expect to cry on TV and I fully expect to experience all of the crushing feelings of disappointment I felt in 2014 and 2018. I *will* crumple – you better believe it.

But the difference is that this time, no matter how much I implode in the aftermath and stand there on TV with tears rolling down my sweaty face, I'll survive.

As much as I might go off the rails for a while, ditch my meds and maybe even self-harm, I will bounce back. And what's more, because I've been open about my mental health struggles, all my friends will be there for me in a way that they couldn't be previously, simply because I'll let them this time.

So, no matter what happens in Beijing, I know that, given time, I'll re-emerge and get on with the rest of my life with a clear conscience, even if, as happens now and again, people shout at me in the street in Nottingham, "You're a flop!" I can take that.

I am, if nothing else, resilient.

I am looking at other careers down the line where I can actively be on hand to help people; jobs such as becoming a paramedic or a career with the police or similar. I'd also like to stay involved in skating on some level going forward. Depending on what happens in Beijing, who knows, I might even skate in the Worlds a month later. Thereafter, while I don't see my individual skating career extending beyond the spring of 2022, I wouldn't rule out skating in mixed relays for a while.

Beyond competition, without sounding too clichéd, I

would really like to give something back to this sport that I call the true love of my life.

Relative to so many others, speed skating just hasn't had the chance to grow in this country in the way that others have. That's a real shame. So many young kids would get a lot out of it, if only there were facilities in place to skate and funding available to support them while they are.

One way or another, whether it be by actively developing a training centre like Nottingham to cover the north, or merely by continuing as a public 'face' of the sport through which to grow it, I'd like to think I'll still be around for a good few years still. I won't be going away, that's for sure.

One last thing though: if you ever see me in the street, be warned. If I'm not wearing any makeup, you're absolutely fine. I'm having a good day.

If I am wearing a lot, stay away! I'm probably having a bad day and my makeup is my way of hiding from the world in plain sight. Given all the hassle I got at school for never wearing any, I know that's a bit ironic. But that mask, that protective barrier between me and the world, is what I need to be resilient every day.